Rev. Caroly Gibson
2/'98 Bethany Retreat
House
Highland Mills, N.Y.

Compass
Retreat w/
Bill
Webber

SURRENDER

A Guide for Prayer

by
Jacqueline Syrup Bergan
S. Marie Schwan

Take and Receive series

Saint Mary's Press
Christian Brothers Publications
Winona, Minnesota

Companion books are available in this Take and Receive series. Write to
Saint Mary's Press
702 Terrace Heights
Winona, MN 55987-1320

All scriptural excerpts are from *The Jerusalem Bible.* Copyright © 1966, by Darton, Longman & Todd, Limited, Doubleday & Company, Inc., used with permission of the publisher.

Selections from *The Spiritual Exercises of St. Ignatius,* translated by David L. Fleming, SJ (The Institute of Jesuit Sources, St. Louis, 1978) are reprinted with permission.

Illustrations and text on pages 92–93 are from the third edition of the *Good News New Testament* in Today's English Version. Copyright © by American Bible Society, 1966, 1971. Used with permission.

Music on page 126 from the Mass for Christian Unity by Jan Vermulst, *People's Mass Book,* copyright © 1966. Used with permission of World Library Publications.

Psalm 22 on page 112 and on 113–115 is from *Psalms Anew: In Inclusive Language* by Nancy Schreck, OSF, and Maureen Leach, OSF. Copyright © 1986 by Saint Mary's Press. Used with permission.

With special thanks to our typist, S. Christine Johnson.

Printed in the United States of America

Printing: 10 9 8

Year: 1996 95

ISBN 0-88489-171-2

think of the love
that
the Father · the Mother ·
have
lavished on us
by
letting us
be called
God's
children

1 John 3:1 (adapted)

to my brother
allen William Syrup

to my sister
Michaela Syrup Key

·Jackie·

to my brother
John Jerome Schwan

·Marie·

Contents

Into Your Hands I Commit My Spirit
Week 6

Abba

Foreword

"Why do people have to suffer?" This question is asked by almost everyone. We may never be able to respond adequately to this question. But still we must pursue the meaning of suffering in our lives, for everything—even suffering—has meaning. Others may say that suffering is absurd, that is, without any meaning at all. But Christians contemplating the suffering and death of Jesus know this is not true.

This fourth volume in the Take and Receive Series, called *Surrender*, will help Christians come to terms with suffering in their lives, not as an end in itself, but as a means to spiritual and holistic growth. The meaning of suffering surfaces, not in denying it or fleeing from it, but in surrendering to it in a prayerful spirit of loving trust in God. This is what we learn from Jesus, who—as he himself said—had to suffer in order to enter into glory (Luke 24:26).

Like the previous volumes in this series, *Surrender* is based on "the living and enduring word of God" (1 Pet. 1:23) and on a mature understanding of the word. I wholeheartedly recommend this volume, then, to all who want God's word to take root in their lives and to blossom, sometimes through suffering, into eternal life.

Victor H. Balke
Bishop of Crookston
Crookston, Minnesota

May 28, 1986

Cover Design

For see, winter is past,
the rains are over and gone.
The flowers appear on the earth.
The season of glad songs has come,
the cooing of the turtledove is heard
in our land.
(Song of Songs 2:11–12)

A "season of glad songs" has begun; throughout the Church is heard the murmur of prayer. Quietly, and in stillness, within the hearts of Christians everywhere, winter has given way to the vitality of spring—the coming of the Spirit.

Among the heralds of spring is the return and nesting of birds. From the days of ancient Israel even to our own times, birds have been symbolic, not only of our deep homing instincts, but also of our creative impulse and of our desire for transcendence.

Frequent allusions to doves are made throughout the Scriptures. In The Song of Songs, the dove announces spring; in Genesis, the olive-bearing dove indicates the end of the flood (Gen. 8:11). At the baptism of Jesus, the presence of the dove initiates a new age of the Spirit (Mark 1:8).

The pair of doves on the cover of volume one, *Love*, symbolizes God's call to love. The cover of volume two, *Forgiveness*, depicts the blessing and nurturing of God's unconditional and forgiving love. The cover of volume three, *Birth*, represents the creative Spirit of God hovering over our world, birthing new life. The empty nest on the cover of this volume, *Surrender*, symbolically conveys the self-emptying love to which Christ submitted himself, in life and death, and to which we as his followers are called.

The mourning dove calls: "Come then, my love. . . . For see, winter is past" (Song of Songs 2:10–11).

The covers were designed by Donna Pierce Campbell, a popular Minnesota artist, whose freshness of style mirrors the spirit of renewal that this guide for prayer hopes to serve.

Introduction

This guide for prayer was inspired by the spiritual hunger we witnessed during the past years as we conducted parish days of renewal throughout northwestern Minnesota.

People shared with us their need and eagerness for guidance and support in developing a personal relationship with God. Gradually we grew in the awareness that for too long the laity has been deprived of resources that are an integral part of the tradition of spirituality within the Church.

One treasure within this tradition is the Spiritual Exercises of Saint Ignatius. The Exercises were a response to the need of the laity in the sixteenth century and have only recently been discovered anew. In the light of Vatican II, with its emphasis on Scripture, interior renewal, and the emergence of the laity, the Exercises have received a new relevance.

As we endeavored to adapt the pattern of the Exercises to parish days of renewal, we discovered an approach for integrating personal prayer with life circumstances that is appropriate to the needs, language, and lifestyle of the laity.

Surrender: A Guide for Prayer is the fourth of five volumes, each of which provides a series of scriptural passages with commentaries and suggested approaches to prayer. The theme of each volume directly correlates with a segment of the Exercises, though each book can be used independently of the others.

The first book in the Take and Receive series, *Love*, makes use of the themes present in the Principle and Foundation of the Spiritual Exercises. Those themes are the affirmation of human creaturehood, indifference to all created things, and commitment. The guide centers on God's love, our total dependence on that love, and the call to respond in freedom to praise, reverence, and serve God.

The second volume, *Forgiveness*, correlates with the first week of the Spiritual Exercises of Saint Ignatius. The themes treat personal and collective sinfulness insofar as it is an obstacle to the receiving of God's love. Sin and sinner are considered in light of God's merciful and forgiving love.

Volume three, *Birth*, is oriented toward a personal discovery of the profound significance of the life of Christ as the paradigm of each one's passage into a way of living that incarnates the Spirit of Jesus in our world. We are invited to contemplate the earthly life of Jesus from his Incarnation throughout his public ministry.

Volume four, *Surrender*, focuses on Christ's total submission to the will of God. Through the contemplation of Jesus' passion and death, his followers are led to an awareness of how suffering can be utilized and transformed. The consideration of paradox is especially significant; in the light of the cross, we encounter the seemingly contradicting elements of our lives, which leads us to a new level of truth and integration. We want to caution those who use this guide for personal prayer and/or in directing others not to be surprised by the heaviness of spirit that may accompany praying through the sufferings and death of Jesus. To prayerfully encounter the passion and surrender of Jesus and our participation in this mystery is not a matter to be taken lightly. The content and symbolism dealt with in this volume are powerful. We recommend that those who undertake this journey have a spiritual friend or director who will walk with them. The prayerful use of this guide will lead to the discovery of how, in and with Christ, personal surrender in suffering is the labor of love, the way, and the power toward union with God and each other.

Written specifically as a support for solitary prayer, the guide can also serve as a resource for faith-sharing in small groups.

The series of guides makes no claim to be the Spiritual Exercises, nor to be a commentary on them. It is an attempt to make available a means of entering into the Christocentric dynamic of conversion found in the Exercises.

In committing this approach to prayer in writing, we hope that more people will be able to draw nourishment from the word of God, experience God's unique love for them, and become aware of the particular intention God holds for each of them.

While we have attempted to be sensitive to the use of inclusive language in the commentaries and approaches to prayer, we have not been entirely consistent. We have been reluctant to make changes in the biblical text out of respect for the word of God and for those people who may find such changes offensive.

Our prayer for those who use this guide is that they will be led by the spirit of Jesus into true spiritual freedom.

May the God of our Lord Jesus Christ, the Father of glory, give you a spirit of wisdom and perception of what is revealed, to bring you to full knowledge of him. • May he enlighten the eyes of your mind so that you can see what hope his call holds for you, what rich glories he has promised the saints will inherit • and how infinitely great is the power that he has exercised for us believers. (Eph. 1:17–19)

Jacqueline Syrup Bergan
S. Marie Schwan

June 1, 1986
Feast of Corpus Christi

Orientations

Lord, teach us to pray. (Luke 11:1)

Prayer is our personal response to God's presence. We approach the Lord reverently with a listening heart. God speaks first. In prayer, we acknowledge the Divine presence and in gratitude respond to God in love. The focus is always on God and on what God does.

The following suggestions are offered as ways of supporting and enabling attentiveness to God's word and our unique response.

A. DAILY PATTERN OF PRAYER

For each period of prayer, use the following pattern:

1. Preparation
- Plan to spend at least twenty minutes to one hour in prayer daily. Though there is nothing "sacred" about sixty minutes, most people find that an hour better provides for the quieting of self, the entrance into the passage, and so on.
- The evening before, take time to read the commentary as well as the scriptural passage for the following day. Just before falling asleep, recall the scriptural passage.

2. Structure of the Prayer Period
- Quiet yourself; be still inside and out. Relax. Breathe in deeply, hold your breath to the count of four, then exhale slowly through your mouth. Repeat several times.
- Realize you are nothing without God; declare your dependency.
- Ask God for the grace you want and need.
- Read and reflect on your chosen scriptural passage, using the appropriate form; for example, use meditation for poetic and nonstory passages, contemplation for story-event passages, and so on. See "Forms of Solitary Prayer," page 2.

1

- Close the prayer period with a time of conversation with Jesus and his Father. Speak and listen. Conclude with an Our Father.

3. Review of Prayer

The review of prayer is a reflection at the conclusion of the prayer period. The purpose of the review is to heighten our awareness of how God has been present to us during the prayer period.

The review focuses primarily on the interior movements of consolation and desolation as they are revealed in our feelings of joy, peace, sadness, fear, ambivalence, anger. Often it is in the review that we become aware of how God has responded to our request for a particular grace.

Writing the review provides for personal accountability and is a precious record of our spiritual journey. To write the review is a step toward self-integration.

In the absence of a spiritual director or a spiritual companion, the writing helps fill the need for evaluation and clarification. If one has a spiritual director, the written review offers an excellent means of preparing to share one's prayer experience.

Method: In a notebook or journal, after each prayer period, indicate the date and the passage. Answer each of the following questions:
- Did any word or phrase particularly strike you?
- What were your feelings? Were you peaceful? loving? trusting? sad? discouraged? What do these feelings say to you?
- How are you more aware of God's presence?
- Would returning to some point be helpful in your next prayer period?

B. FORMS OF SOLITARY PRAYER

Scriptural prayer has various forms, and different forms appeal to different people. Eventually, by trying various methods, we become adept at using approaches that are appropriate to particular passages and are in harmony with our personality and needs.

This guide will make use of the following forms:

1. Meditation

In meditation one approaches the scriptural passage like a love letter; this approach is especially helpful in praying poetic passages.

Method:
- Read the passage slowly, aloud or in a whisper, letting the words wash over you and savoring them.
- Stay with the words that especially catch your attention; absorb them the way the thirsty earth receives the rain.
- Keep repeating a word or phrase, aware of the feelings that are awakened.
- Read and reread the passage lovingly as you would a letter from a dear friend, or as you would softly sing the chorus of a song.

2. Contemplation

In contemplation, we enter into a life event or story passage of Scripture. We enter into the passage by way of imagination, making use of all our senses.

Theologians tell us that through contemplation we are able to "recall and be present at the mysteries of Christ's life" (26, p. 149).

The Spirit of Jesus, present within us through baptism, teaches us, just as Jesus taught the Apostles. The Spirit recalls and enlivens the particular mystery into which we enter through prayer. Just as in the Eucharist the Risen Jesus makes present the paschal mystery, in contemplation he brings forward the particular event we are contemplating and presents himself within that mystery.

Method: In contemplation, one enters the story as if one were there.
- Watch what happens; listen to what is being said.
- Become part of the mystery; assume the role of one of the persons.
- Look at each of the individuals; what does he or she experience? To whom does each one speak?
- What difference does it make for my life, my family, for society, if I hear the message?

In the gospel stories, enter into dialogue with Jesus.
- *Be there* with him and for him.
- *Want him;* hunger for him.

3

- *Listen* to him.
- *Let him* be for you what he wants to be.
- *Respond to him* (73, pp. 5–6).

3. Centering Prayer

"In centering prayer we go beyond thought and image, beyond the senses and the rational mind to that center of our being where God is working a wonderful work" (61, p. 28).

Centering prayer is a very simple, pure form of prayer, frequently without words; it is an opening of our hearts to the Spirit dwelling within us.

In centering prayer, we spiral down into the deepest center of ourselves. It is the point of stillness within us where we most experience being created by a loving God who is breathing us into life. To enter into centering prayer requires a recognition of our dependency on God and a surrender to God's Spirit of love.

"The Spirit too comes to help us in our weakness. . . . the Spirit . . . expresses our plea in a way that could never be put into words . . ." (Rom. 8:26).

The Spirit of Jesus within us cries out "Abba, Father!" (Rom. 8:15).

Method: "Pause a while and know that I am God . . . " (Ps. 46:10).
- Sit quietly, comfortable and relaxed.
- Rest within your longing and desire for God.
- Move to the center within your deepest self. To facilitate this movement, image yourself slowly descending in an elevator, or walking down flights of stairs, or descending a mountain, or going down into the water, as in a deep pool.
- In the stillness, become aware of God's presence; peacefully absorb God's love.

4. Mantra

One means of centering prayer is the use of the "mantra" or "prayer word." The mantra can be a single word or a phrase. It may be a word from Scripture or one that arises spontaneously from within your heart. The word or phrase represents, for you, the fullness of God.

4

Variations of the mantra may include the name "Jesus" or what is known as the Jesus prayer, "Lord, Jesus Christ, Son of the living God, have mercy on me, a sinner."

Method: Repeat the word or phrase slowly within yourself in harmony with your breathing. For example, say the first part of the Jesus prayer while inhaling; say the second half while exhaling.

5. Meditative Reading

"I opened my mouth; he gave me the scroll to eat • and said, '. . . feed and be satisfied by the scroll I am giving you.' I ate it, and it tasted sweet as honey" (Ezek. 3:2–3).

One of the approaches to prayer is a reflective reading of Scripture or other spiritual writings.

Spiritual reading is always enriching to our life of prayer. The method described below is especially supportive in times when prayer is difficult or dry.

Method: Read slowly, pausing periodically to allow the words and phrases to enter within you. When a thought resonates deeply, stay with it, allowing the fullness of it to penetrate your being. Relish the word received. Respond authentically and spontaneously as in a dialogue.

6. Journaling

"If you read my words, you will have some idea of the depths that I see in the mystery of Christ" (Eph. 3:4).

Journaling is meditative writing. When we place pen on paper, spirit and body cooperate to release our true selves.

There is a difference between journaling and keeping a journal.

To journal is to experience ourselves in a new light as expression is given to the fresh images which emerge from our subconscious. Journaling requires putting aside preconceived ideas and control.

Meditative writing is like writing a letter to one we love. We recall memories, clarify convictions, and our affections well up within us. In writing we may discover that emotions are intensified and prolonged.

5

Because of this, journaling can also serve in identifying and healing hidden, suppressed emotions such as anger, fear, and resentment.

Finally, journaling can give us a deeper appreciation for the written word as we encounter it in Scripture.

Method: Among the many variations of journaling in prayer are the following:

- writing a letter addressed to God;
- writing a conversation between oneself and another (The other may be Jesus, or another significant person. The dialogue can also be with an event, an experience, or a value. For example, death, separation, or wisdom receives personal attributes and is imaged as a person with whom one enters into conversation);
- writing an answer to a question; for example, "What do you want me to do for you?" (Mark 10:51) or "Why are you weeping?" (John 20:15);
- allowing Jesus or another Scripture person to "speak" to us through the pen. ans. your letter w/ opposite hand

7. Repetition

"I will remain quietly meditating upon the point in which I have found what I desire without any eagerness to go on till I have been satisfied" (Saint Ignatius of Loyola; 73, p. 110).

Repetition is the return to a previous period of prayer for the purpose of allowing the movements of God to deepen within one's heart.

Through repetitions, we fine-tune our sensitivities to God and to how God speaks in our prayer and within our life circumstances. The prayer of repetition allows for the experience of integrating who we are with who God is revealing himself to be for us.

Repetition is a way of honoring God's word to us in the earlier prayer period. It is recalling and pondering an earlier conversation with one we love. It is as if we say to God, "Tell me that again; what did I hear you saying?"

In this follow-up conversation or repetition, we open ourselves to a healing presence that often transforms whatever sadness and confusion we may have experienced in the first prayer.

In repetitions, not only is the consolation (joy, warmth, peace) deepened, but the desolation (pain, sadness, confusion) is frequently brought to a new level of understanding and acceptance within God's plan for us.

Method: The period of prayer that we select to repeat is one in which we have experienced a significant movement of joy or sadness or confusion. It may also be a period in which nothing seemed to happen, due, perhaps, to our own lack of readiness at the time.

- Recall the feelings of the first period of prayer.
- As a point of entry, use the scene, word, or feeling that was previously most significant.
- Allow the Spirit to direct the inner movements of your heart during this time of prayer.

C. SPIRITUAL PRACTICES AND HELPS

1. Examen of Consciousness
"Yahweh, you examine me and know me . . ." (Ps. 139:1).

The examen of consciousness is the instrument by which we discover how God has been present to us and how we have responded to that presence through the day.

Saint Ignatius believed this practice was so important that, in the event it was impossible to have a formal prayer period, he insisted that the examen would sustain one's vital link with God.

The examen of consciousness is not to be confused with an examination of conscience in which penitents are concerned with their failures. It is, rather, an exploration of how God is present within the events, circumstances, feelings of our daily lives.

What the review is to the prayer period, the examen is to our daily life. The daily discipline of an authentic practice of the examen effects the integrating balance which is essential for growth in relationship to God, to self, and to others.

The method reflects the "dynamic movement of personal love: what we always want to say to a person whom we truly love in the order in which we want

7

*

to say it. . . . Thank you. . . . Help me. . . . I love you. . . . I'm sorry. . . . Be with me" (19, pp. 34–35).

Method: The following prayer is a suggested approach to examen. You can incorporate the written response into the prayer journal.

[handwritten left margin: Silence after each — S. me speak aloud]

- God, my Creator, I am totally dependent on you. Everything is a gift from you. *All is gift.* I give you thanks and praise for the gifts of this day. . . .
- Lord, I believe you work through and in time to reveal me to myself. Please give me an increased awareness of how you are guiding and shaping my life, as well as a more sensitive awareness of the obstacles I put in your way.
- You have been present in my life today. Be near, now, as I reflect on these things:
  your presence in the *events* of today . . .
  your presence in the *feelings* I experienced today . . .
  your *call* to me . . .
  my *response* to you . . .
- God, I ask your loving forgiveness and healing. The particular event of this day that I most want healed is . . .
- Filled with hope and a firm belief in your love and power, I entrust myself to your care and strongly affirm . . . (Claim the gift you most desire, most need; believe that God desires to give you that gift.)

2. Faith-Sharing *small cov. groups*

"For where two or three meet in my name, I shall be there with them" (Matt. 18:20).

In the creation of community, members must communicate intimately with each other about the core issues of their lives. For the Christian, this is faith-sharing and is an extension of daily solitary prayer.

A faith-sharing group is not a discussion group, not a sensitivity session nor a social gathering. Members do not come together to share and receive intellectual or theological insights. Nor is the purpose of faith-sharing the accomplishment of some predetermined task.

Disciples of Jesus Continuing The Ministries of Jesus

Being Jesus people Doing Jesus things

The purpose of faith-sharing is to listen and to be open to God, who continues to reveal himself in the Church community represented in the small group which comes together in God's name. The fruit of faith-sharing is the "building up" of the Church, the Body of Christ (Eph. 4:12).

The approach to faith-sharing is one of reading and reflecting together on the Word of God. Faith-sharing calls us to share with each other, out of our deepest center, what it means to be a follower of Christ in our world today. To authentically enter into faith-sharing is to come to know and love each other in Christ whose Spirit is the bonding force of community.

An image that faith-sharing groups may find helpful is that of a pool into which pebbles are dropped. The group gathers in a circle imaging themselves around a pool. Like a pebble being gently dropped into the water, each one offers a reflection—his or her "word" from God. In the shared silence, each offering is received. As the water ripples in concentric circles toward the outer reaches of the pool, so too this word enlarges and embraces, in love, each member of the circle.

Method: A group of seven to ten members gathers at a prearranged time and place.

- The leader calls the group to prayer and invites members to some moments of silent centering, during which they pray for the presence of the Holy Spirit.
- The leader gathers their silent prayer in an opening prayer, spontaneous or prepared.

May use at B.S.

- One of the members reads a previously chosen scriptural passage on which participants have spent some time in solitary prayer.
- A period of silence follows each reading of the Scripture.
- The leader invites each one to share a word or phrase from the reading.
- Another member rereads the passage; this is followed by a time of silence.
- The leader invites those who wish, to share how this passage personally addresses them, for example, by challenging, comforting, inviting.
- Again the passage is read.
- Members are invited to offer their spontaneous prayer to the Lord.
- The leader draws the time of faith-sharing to closure with a prayer, a blessing, an Our Father, or a hymn.

9

- Before the group disbands, the passage for the following session is announced.

3. The Role of Imagination in Prayer

Imagination is our power of memory and recall which enables us to enter into the experience of the past and to create the future. Through images we are able to touch the center of who we are and to surface and give life and expression to the innermost levels of our being.

The use of images is important to our psycho-spiritual development. Images simultaneously reveal multiple levels of meaning and are therefore symbolic of our deeper reality.

Through the structured use of active imagination, we release the hidden energy and potential for wholeness which is already present within us.

When we use active imagination in the context of prayer, and with an attitude of faith, we open ourselves to the power and mystery of God's transforming presence within us.

Because Scripture is, for the most part, a collection of stories and rich in sensual imagery, the use of active imagination in praying Scripture is particularly enriching.

Through imaging Scripture we go beyond the truth of history to discover the truth of the mystery of God's creative word in our lives (21, p. 76).

4. Coping with Distractions

Do not become overly concerned or discouraged by distractions during prayer. Simply put them aside and return to your prayer material. If and when a distraction persists, it may be a call to attend prayerfully to the object of the distraction. For example, an unresolved conflict may well continue to surface until it has been dealt with.

5. Colloquy: Closing Conversational Prayer

Saint Ignatius is very sensitive to the depth of feeling aroused by the contemplation of the suffering of Jesus. While a suggestion for this intimate conversational prayer at the end of each prayer period has been provided, the pray-er is encouraged to let his or her heart speak in an intimate outpouring of feeling, of love and compassion. The pray-er is strongly urged to *be with* Jesus in His suffering. Sometimes the closing conversational prayer will provide an opportunity for one to pour out his or her discouragement, temptation, fear or to express the difficulty in entering into the suffering of Christ. One may need to pray for the desire to *want* to experience suffering with Christ. The important thing to remember is that simple presence is what is primary. Just to be silent in the presence of Christ's suffering is profound prayer.

Prayer of Love and Praise

Lord my God, when Your love spilled over
        into creation
                You thought of me.
             I am
from love   of love   for love.

Let my heart, O God, always
        recognize,
        cherish,
        and enjoy your goodness in all of creation.

Direct all that is me toward your praise.
Teach me reverence for every person, all things.
Energize me in your service

              Lord God
may nothing ever distract me from your
        love . . .
              neither health nor sickness
                wealth nor poverty
                honor nor dishonor
                long life nor short life.

May I never seek nor choose to be other
        than You intend or wish.   Amen.

Week 1, Day 1: The Power and the Possibility

LUKE 9:23–27

Then to all he said, "If anyone wants to be a follower of mine, let him renounce himself and take up his cross every day and follow me. • For anyone who wants to save his life will lose it; but anyone who loses his life for my sake, that [one] will save it. • What gain, then, is it for a [person] to have won the whole world and to have lost or ruined his very self? • For if anyone is ashamed of me and of my words, of him the Son of Man will be ashamed when he comes in his own glory and in the glory of the Father and the holy angels.

"I tell you truly, there are some standing here who will not taste death before they see the kingdom of God."

"I'll never forget the first time I heard that the resurrection of Jesus was to be experienced *now*, in the present," a friend shared. "It was a moment of heightened realization when suddenly, in a new way, I grasped the power and the possibility of the Risen Christ within me. For days I walked in stunned awareness, knowing that I need not wait until death to experience the wonder of his spirit."

This reality of Jesus Risen is the most astounding gift a loving creator could give his human creatures. And we, as post-resurrection people, find in Jesus Risen the power and direction for our lives.

Luke's instruction to the early Christian community on discipleship must be read within the context of this living awareness of the resurrection.

In Jesus' own words, Luke imparts to us the heart and mind we are to nurture if we are to become authentic disciples of Christ.

Jesus presents us with a demanding challenge. He is insistent on unwavering loyalty. No one, no thing, no circumstance, embarrassment, or shame can be allowed to deflect us from the priority of following him.

And, *all* are called! By reason of baptism this radical demand is inherent to each Christian journey.

Yet, within this unrelenting call is the freedom of choice. That choice is undeniably mirrored in our response to the simple question, *"How have I loved?"* The answer will reveal whether we have been self- or other-centered. In our seeking to find our truest selves have our efforts and activities been directed primarily toward self-enhancement and security, or has our journey toward wholeness led us to an active loving concern for others?

Luke presents us with "the most fundamental paradox of Jesus' teaching: a life bent on personal survival is a life lost," but a life lost and given in loving service is a life saved (43, p. 132).

To say yes to this call to discipleship is to commit oneself to a complete orientation to the way of Christ. To follow Christ is to embrace life in its totality with all its joys, successes, failures, and disappointments; it is to concretely and to daily encounter life's ambiguities, tensions, and paradoxes. To be a disciple of Christ is to courageously risk a sensitive and open response to the rhythm of light and darkness as it moves and shapes the reality of our lives.

Jesus says, "If anyone wants to be a follower of mine, let him renounce himself and take up his cross every day and follow me" (Matt. 16:24).

The Gospel invites us to assume our *own* cross as the circumstances and situations of our lives reveal it to us.

To follow Christ means to claim one's own particular destiny, just as Christ claimed his own unique identity and mission. Discipleship of Jesus exemplifies the paradox of all authentic relationships—one stands alone, yet is mysteriously united with Christ.

The way of Christ is the way of love. This way of love is the yoke of life, the supportive, balancing, enablement of the Spirit that empowered Jesus and, in turn, empowers us. To share that yoke of life releases the unlimited possibilities of creativity, joy, and fulfillment that are at the heart of discipleship.

"Come to me all you who labor and are overburdened. . . . Shoulder my yoke and learn from me, for I am gentle and humble in heart. . . . Yes, my yoke is easy and my burden light" (Matt. 11:28–30).

Suggested Approach to Prayer: Personally Invited

+ *Daily prayer pattern:* (See pages 1 and 2.)

14

I quiet myself and relax in the presence of God.
I declare my dependency on God.

+ *Grace:* I ask to know and love Jesus more intimately so that I may follow him in faith and with courage.

+ *Method:* Contemplation, as on page 3.

I image myself walking and coming upon Jesus and his disciples. He invites me to sit with them. I am attentive to the kind of day it is, whether it's sunny or overcast, warm or chilly. I am aware of the disciples, their response to my presence, and if they welcome me.

I settle myself in quietness and listen very closely to the words of Jesus. I watch his expression as he speaks. I am aware of how he is firm or gentle, consoling or demanding. I allow his words to resonate deeply within me. I am keenly aware of the response his words precipitate within me.

When Jesus finishes speaking and the disciples leave, I image myself remaining behind. Jesus approaches me and speaks his invitation to discipleship directly to me.

I share with him my feelings about saying yes to becoming his disciple, for example, excitement, fear, confusion, urgency, anticipation.

+ *Closing:* I speak my heart's desires to Jesus. I listen to his words to me. I pray the Our Father.

+ *Review of Prayer:* In my journal I record the feelings and responses that surfaced during my prayer.

Week 1, Day 2: Inexpressible Joy

LUKE 9:28–36

Now about eight days after this had been said, he took with him Peter and John and James and went up the mountain to pray. • As he prayed, the aspect of his face was changed and his clothing became brilliant as lightning. • Suddenly there were two men there talking to him; they were Moses and Elijah • appearing in glory, and they were speaking of his passing which he was to accomplish in Jerusalem. • Peter and his companions were heavy with sleep, but they kept awake and saw his glory and the two men standing with him. • As these were leaving him, Peter said to Jesus, "Master, it is wonderful for us to be here; so let us make three tents, one for you, one for Moses and one for Elijah."—He did not know what he was saying. • As he spoke, a cloud came and covered them with shadow; and when they went into the cloud the disciples were afraid. • And a voice came from the cloud saying, "This is my Son, the Chosen One. Listen to him." • And after the voice had spoken, Jesus was found alone. The disciples kept silence and, at that time, told no one what they had seen.

In each of our lives are heightened moments of joy and awareness that forever elude adequate expression. Attempts to share these experiences fall short. Our words seem flat and empty, unable to hold the transcendent fullness of the event. We search for images, for symbols that have the collective efficacy to convey our enthusiasm and insight.

"Let us make three tents!"

Peter was overcome with awe and joy in the presence of the glory of God shining forth in his friend and leader, Jesus. In his great joy, he impulsively cried out, "Let us make three tents!"

Instinctively and spontaneously Peter drew upon one of the greatest expressions of joy his people experienced, the annual communal celebration of the Feast of Tents, the Feast of Tabernacles.

Each year the Jewish people looked forward to this great festival. After the autumn harvest they came in one great pilgrimage to the sanctuary to offer praise and thanksgiving for God's abundant goodness to them and to ask the Lord to send rains for the coming year.

To accommodate the many people, small booths—"tents"—were constructed wherever there was space, on hillsides and housetops, and in the corners of courtyards. The booths were made of palm branches and decorated with fruit.

There was little time for sleeping during the joyous week-long festival. The entire time was given over to merriment and praise.

The Jewish people knew how to celebrate! Magnificent processions began early in the morning, each participant carrying a palm branch and singing praise. Throughout the night, men danced in the sanctuary courtyard, dressed in white garments and carrying lighted torches.

The memories of the splendor of this great feast sustained and nurtured the Jewish people throughout the entire year.

Peter's notion to build three tents—one for Jesus, one for Moses, and one for Elijah—gave voice to the deeper reality of his desire to prolong, to celebrate, and to mark the great moment of Jesus' transfiguration.

In using the symbolism associated with the Feast of Tents, Luke is endeavoring to convey something of the mystery of God's presence made visible in Jesus.

What *did* Peter and his companions hear? What *did* they see?

They saw Moses and Elijah converse with Jesus about the necessity of Jesus' own exodus, that is, his imminent suffering, death, and glorification. They saw the prophets of the Jewish Scriptures depart and give way to the new hope held in following Jesus. The disciples were privileged to receive a sustaining glimpse of the glory of Jesus' resurrection.

Peter, James, and John heard again the words spoken at Jesus' baptism, "This is my son, the Chosen One." The voice definitively confirmed the identity of Jesus as God's Son and as God's divinely elected suffering servant (Isa. 42:1).

Then, enveloped by the awesome cloud of God's presence, the disciples received the instruction, "Listen to him."

Later, in the absence of Jesus' physical presence, the disciples, committed by faith, would discover meaning for their lives and direction for their mission through a dedicated adherence to, and dependency on, the gospel word.

"After the voice had spoken, Jesus was found alone."

The mountain of transfiguration leads to the mount of Calvary.

On the mount of transfiguration Jesus was prepared to "resolutely" take the road to Jerusalem, city of his destiny (Luke 9:51). Confirmed in faith, the disciples would follow.

Like Peter, James, and John, we, too, join our voices with those of ancient Israel, who on the Feast of Tabernacles sang their praise and gratitude to God.

This is the day made memorable by Yahweh,
>   what immense joy for us! . . .
Give thanks to Yahweh, for he is good,
>   his love is everlasting.

>   (Ps. 118:24, 29)

Suggested Approach to Prayer: The Enveloping Cloud

+ *Daily prayer pattern:* (See pages 1 and 2.)
I quiet myself and relax in the presence of God.
I declare my dependency on God.

+ *Grace:* I ask to know and love Jesus more intimately so that I may follow him in faith and with courage.

+ *Method:* Contemplation, as on page 3.
I image myself being invited by Jesus to accompany him with Peter, James, and John to the mountain.

As I climb, I consider in detail the arduous task I am undertaking, pausing frequently to observe the changing perspective of the terrain below.

As we reach the summit, I am aware of Jesus and the disciples as they quiet themselves in prayer. I relax and enter into prayer.

I contemplate Jesus in prayer as he enters deeply into communion with

18

God. I see this union of love reflected in his face, his posture, in his total demeanor.

I allow myself to absorb this glory of God in Jesus.

I become aware of the presence of Moses and Elijah and listen carefully to their conversation with Jesus.

As the event unfolds, I am drawn into Peter's excitement and desire to remain here.

I become aware of the cloud of God's presence enveloping us all. I listen and am aware of my own feeling response as I hear addressed to me the words, "This is my Son, the Chosen One. Listen to him."

+ *Closing:* Alone with Jesus, I let my heart express my gratitude.
I pray the Our Father.

+ *Review of Prayer:* I record in my journal the thoughts and feelings that surfaced during my prayer.

Week 1, Day 3: Awakening

JOHN 11:1–44

There was a man named Lazarus who lived in the village of Bethany with the two sisters, Mary and Martha, and he was ill. —• *It was the same Mary, the sister of the sick man Lazarus, who anointed the Lord with ointment and wiped his feet with her hair.* • *The sisters sent this message to Jesus, "Lord, the man you love is ill."* • *On receiving the message, Jesus said, "This sickness will end, not in death but in God's glory, and through it the Son of God will be glorified."*

Jesus loved Martha and her sister and Lazarus, • *yet when he heard that Lazarus was ill he stayed where he was for two more days* • *before saying to the disciples, "Let us go to Judaea."* • *The disciples said, "Rabbi, it is not long since the Jews wanted to stone you; are you going back again?"* • *Jesus replied:*

"Are there not twelve hours in the day?
A man can walk in the daytime without stumbling
because he has the light of this world to see by;
but if he walks at night, he stumbles,
because there is no light to guide him."

He said that and then added, "Our friend Lazarus is resting, and I am going to wake him." • *The disciples said to him, "Lord, if he is able to rest he is sure to get better."* • *The phrase Jesus used referred to the death of Lazarus, but they thought that by "rest" he meant "sleep," so* • *Jesus put it plainly, "Lazarus is dead;* • *and for your sake I am glad I was not there because now you will believe. But let us go to him."* • *Then Thomas—known as the Twin—said to the other disciples, "Let us go too, and die with him."*

On arriving, Jesus found that Lazarus had been in the tomb for four days already. • Bethany is only about two miles from Jerusalem, • and many Jews had come to Martha and Mary to sympathize with them over their brother. • When Martha heard that Jesus had come she went to meet him. Mary remained sitting in the house. • Martha said to Jesus, "If you had been here, my brother would not have died, • but I know that, even now, whatever you ask of God, he will grant you." • "Your brother" said Jesus to her "will rise again." • Martha said, "I know he will rise again at the resurrection on the last day." • Jesus said:

"I am the resurrection.
If anyone believes in me, even though he dies he will live,
and whoever lives and believes in me
will never die.
Do you believe this?"

"Yes, Lord," she said "I believe that you are the Christ, the Son of God, the one who was to come into this world."

When she had said this, she went and called her sister Mary, saying in a low voice, "The Master is here and wants to see you." • Hearing this, Mary got up quickly and went to him. • Jesus had not yet come into the village; he was still at the place where Martha had met him. • When the Jews who were in the house sympathizing with Mary saw her get up so quickly and go out, they followed her, thinking that she was going to the tomb to weep there.

Mary went to Jesus, and as soon as she saw him she threw herself at his feet, saying, "Lord, if you had been here, my brother would not have died." • At the sight of her tears, and those of the Jews who followed her, Jesus said in great distress, with a sigh that came straight from the heart, • "Where have you put him!" They said, "Lord, come and see."

• *Jesus wept;* • *and the Jews said, "See how much he loved him!"* • *But there were some who remarked, "He opened the eyes of the blind man, could he not have prevented this man's death?"* • *Still sighing, Jesus reached the tomb: it was a cave with a stone to close the opening. Jesus said, "Take the stone away." Martha said to him, "Lord, by now he will smell; this is the fourth day."* • *Jesus replied, "Have I not told you that if you believe you will see the glory of God?"* • *So they took away the stone. Then Jesus lifted up his eyes and said:*

> *"Father, I thank you for hearing my prayer.*
> *I knew indeed that you always hear me,*
> *but I speak*
> *for the sake of all these who stand round me,*
> *so that they may believe it was you who sent me."*

> *When he had said this, he cried in a loud voice, "Lazarus, here! Come out!"* • *The dead man came out, his feet and hands bound with bands of stuff and a cloth round his face. Jesus said to them, "Unbind him, let him go free."*

Lazarus haunts us!

In him we see our own story. Like Lazarus we sleep, entombed in lethargy, loneliness, self-centeredness, and fear.

We are asleep! This is *our* "tragedy."

In his play *Lazarus Laughed*, Eugene O'Neill ingeniously portrays the inescapable struggle to affirm life within death, creation within chaos (Gen. 1:2).

"That is your tragedy! You forget! You forget the God in you!" (58, act 1, scene 2, 189).

The sleep into which we escape is the sleep from life. It is, essentially, a denial of life. Isolation, withdrawal, and unbelief serve as the harbingers of this winter season of meaninglessness.

We allow inertia to imprison us, and rather than trusting ourselves to the risks and joys of life, we choose the deceptive comfort of "sleep." In so doing, we precipitate our own catatonic death.

"You wish to forget! Remembrance would imply the high duty to live as the son of God—generously!—with love!—with pride!—with laughter!" (ibid.).

Jesus is the link from death to life. Just as clearly as he called to his friend, "Lazarus, here! Come out!" he calls us.

Come out!

We hear his voice whenever we are attentive. It reaches deep within our entombment. We need not wait for physical death. Belief in Jesus, obedience to his words, is our passage, *now*, into eternal life.

Lazarus is the sign that the power in Jesus is what raises life out of death. Neither belief in Jesus as the "miracle worker" nor belief in the resurrection is the key that opens the way to life. Rather, it is belief in Jesus, himself, as God's son (62, p. 171).

The fullness of being, already present within, awaits only our yes to the person of Jesus.

To be awakened from the sleep of self is to be plunged into an acute awareness of life, into all its paradoxes of suffering and hope. It allows no escape from the harsh reality of an ailing world intent on death.

"It is a world dead to . . . joy. . . . Its will is so sick that it must kill in order to be aware of life at all" (58, act 3, scene 1, 330).

It is into this world of rejection and unbelief that Jesus came. In the giving of life to Lazarus, Jesus was setting the stage for his own death, resurrection, and glorification. Jesus had no escape, and there will be none for us: the way to life is the way of Jesus. That way is the paradoxical path of self-giving; it is laying down one's life for others (John 12:24-25; 15:13).

Jesus is the resounding yes of the Father.

In Jesus the future is made present, the end is now. The awakening of Lazarus is the promise and joy of new life for us.

And Lazarus laughed!

"I heard the heart of Jesus laughing in my heart. . . . And my heart reborn to love of life cried, Yes! And I laughed in the laughter of God!" (58, act 1, scene 1, 279).

Suggested Approach to Prayer: "Come Out"

+ *Daily prayer pattern:* (See pages 1 and 2.)
I quiet myself and relax in the presence of God.
I declare my dependency on God.

+ *Grace:* I ask to know and love Jesus more intimately so that I may follow him in faith and with courage.

+ *Method:* Contemplation, as on page 3.
I image myself, like Lazarus, entombed.
I allow myself to experience the darkness, the damp chill, the aloneness, the confinement. I become aware of the walls of my tomb.
I consider prayerfully what it is in me that has given shape to the stones that form my prison.
I ask myself if the stones are those of apathy, self-centeredness, fear, distrust, self-doubt, culpable ignorance, unhealed memories . . .
I particularize my tomb by writing on each of the stones the name which gives it form.
I focus my attention on the large entrance stone blocking my freedom.
In my aloneness I listen expectantly for the voice of Jesus calling me to "come out." I hear him address me by name. "_____, come out."
I use these words as a mantra (page 4), hearing them over and over, resounding in my heart.
I allow these words of Jesus to penetrate the large stone and to call me forth into freedom of life with him. I allow him to unbind and free me.

+ *Closing:* I ask Mary to intercede for me that I would receive the gift of total dependency on God. I ask that I would be so detached from all things that I would put all my talents, possessions, and achievements at the service of Christ. I pray to follow in the pattern of Christ's life—even to the end. Providing it would not be sinful on anyone's part, I pray that if it is God's wish for me, I would have, like Christ, the courage and strength to endure poverty and/or personal humiliation.
I pray the Hail Mary.
In the company of Mary, I approach Jesus and offer the same prayer, that

he would obtain these graces for me from my Creator. I pray "Soul of Christ," p. 138.

In the presence of Jesus and Mary, and offered by them, I approach God my Creator. Again I make the same request.

I pray the Our Father.

+ *Review of Prayer:* I write in my journal what has surfaced in my prayer, attending especially to the feelings that were present.

Week 1, Day 4: More Than He Knew

JOHN 11:45–54

Many of the Jews who had come to visit Mary and had seen what he did believed in him, • but some of them went to tell the Pharisees what Jesus had done. • Then the chief priests and Pharisees called a meeting. "Here is this man working all these signs" they said "and what action are we taking? • If we let him go on in this way everybody will believe in him, and the Romans will come and destroy the Holy Place and our nation." • One of them, Caiaphas, the high priest that year, said, "You don't seem to have grasped the situation at all; • you fail to see that it is better for one man to die for the people, than for the whole nation to be destroyed." • He did not speak in his own person, it was as high priest that he made this prophecy that Jesus was to die for the nation—• and not for the nation only, but to gather together in unity the scattered children of God. • From that day they were determined to kill him. • So Jesus no longer went about openly among the Jews, but left the district for a town called Ephraim, in the country bordering on the desert, and stayed there with his disciples.

He didn't know what he was saying!

"It is better for one man to die for the people, than for the whole nation to be destroyed."

Ironically, the words which articulated and set into motion the final liberating act of Jesus came from the lips of the leader of the opposition, Caiaphas.

High priest in that crucial year, Caiaphas spoke out of political expediency. He was under strong pressure to subdue Jesus.

Fearing the destruction of the temple by the Romans, he failed to perceive that he himself was contributing to its collapse. He was unable to make the leap of faith that would have allowed him to see Jesus as the new temple (John 2:19). Unfortunately there were those among his followers who joined him in the rejection of Jesus.

Unaware of the profound ramifications of his words, Caiaphas paradoxically effected the fulfillment of Jesus' mission.

The early Christian community remembered the episode of this preliminary trial of Jesus as the unconscious prophecy of the high priest, Caiaphas.

In less than six months, Jesus had given the people two major signs of God's love. He gave sight to the man born blind (John 9) and he raised Lazarus from the dead (John 11:1–44).

Some believed; some did not believe.

Because some believed, Jesus had to die. The enthusiasm Jesus aroused threatened those in authority and was the catalytic force that led to his death. The ultimate irony was that the death of Jesus gave birth to the very thing the Pharisees sought to eliminate, the creation of a new community!

Jesus died "not for the nation only, but to gather together in unity the scattered children of God." God's love, made visible in Jesus' dying for all of humankind, enfolded Gentile as well as Jew into the new Israel, the Church. Caiaphas truly said more than he knew!

Suggested Approach to Prayer: Response to Jesus

+ *Daily prayer pattern:* (See pages 1 and 2.)
    I quiet myself and relax in the presence of God.
    I declare my dependency on God.

+ *Grace:* I ask to know and love Jesus more intimately so that I may follow him in faith and with courage.

+ *Method:* Contemplation, as on page 3.
    As I recall the signs of Jesus' power, I image again the persons whose lives were transformed through his compassionate love: the man born blind who was given sight, the woman cured of the hemorrhage, Lazarus raised from the dead. . .
    I place myself in the crowd of onlookers who witness these signs of power.

I look at the people present to see if they are angry, doubtful, threatened, excited, joyous. . .

I especially consider how the witnesses respond to the person of Jesus.

I note that some believe and others do not. I am aware of my own heart's response to Jesus.

I image myself present at the impromptu gathering of the chief priests and Pharisees.

I listen attentively to the charges leveled at Jesus.

I hear the elders express their intent to execute Jesus.

I become acutely aware of my own feeling responses to the Pharisees' accusations and their plot to kill Jesus.

I consider prayerfully that I am among those "people" for whom Jesus died.

+ *Closing:* I ask Mary to intercede for me that I would receive the gift of total dependency on God. I ask that I would be so detached from all things that I would put all my talents, possessions, and achievements at the service of Christ. I pray to follow in the pattern of Christ's life—even to the end. Providing it would not be sinful on anyone's part, I pray that if it is God's wish for me, I would have, like Christ, the courage and strength to endure poverty and/or personal humiliation.

I pray the Hail Mary.

In the company of Mary, I approach Jesus and offer the same prayer, that he would obtain these graces for me from my Creator. I pray "Soul of Christ," p. 138.

In the presence of Jesus and Mary, and offered by them, I approach God my Creator. Again I make the same request.

I pray the Our Father.

+ *Review of Prayer:* I write in my journal what has surfaced in my prayer, attending especially to the feelings that were present.

Week 1, Day 5: Anointed with Love

JOHN 12:1–8

Six days before the Passover, Jesus went to Bethany, where Lazarus was, whom he had raised from the dead. • They gave a dinner for him there; Martha waited on them and Lazarus was among those at table. • Mary brought in a pound of very costly ointment, pure nard, and with it anointed the feet of Jesus, wiping them with her hair; the house was full of the scent of the ointment. • Then Judas Iscariot—one of his disciples, the man who was to betray him—said, • "Why wasn't this ointment sold for three hundred denarii, and the money given to the poor?" • He said this, not because he cared about the poor, but because he was a thief; he was in charge of the common fund and used to help himself to the contributions. • So Jesus said, "Leave her alone; she had to keep this scent for the day of my burial. • You have the poor with you always, you will not always have me."

"The house was full of the scent of the ointment."

An extraordinary thing happened when Jesus returned to Bethany. There was a moment so exquisitely beautiful that it was nearly inexpressible. It was one of those rare moments when a person is so overwhelmed with love for another that all reservations and self-consciousness fall away as if no one else were present, and love overflows in a fullness of expression.

The moment at Bethany occurred when, with precious and costly ointment, Mary anointed the feet of Jesus.

Mary responded simply and spontaneously from her deep love for Jesus. At the same time, her instinctive action also revealed her subconscious love-knowledge of Jesus.

In anointing Jesus' feet, Mary did something culturally inappropriate; feet were anointed only as part of the embalming ritual. Thus, her expression of love, the act of anointing, was a transparent prophecy of Jesus' imminent death.

Jesus acknowledged it; "she had to keep this scent for the day of my burial."

The house was filled with the fragrance of the perfume.

Throughout the centuries, those who believe have remembered and celebrated the beauty of this moment. The scent which permeated the house has come to symbolize, for those who deeply love him, the essence of Jesus' glorious presence permeating the entire world. "His glory fills the whole earth" (Isa. 6:3).

Unfortunately, not all who witnessed the moment were open to seeing this glory. Judas was blind to it, his mind warped by the shadow of darkness. While those who believed saw a supreme expression of love, Judas saw only a rash extravagance, foolish and wasteful.

The contrast between Mary, who loved, and Judas, who did not believe, is striking!

One in the crowd saw clearly the intent and full import of Mary's gesture of love. That one was Jesus. He countered Judas' disgruntled criticism with the reprimand, "Leave her alone. . . . You have the poor with you always; you will not always have me."

Jesus was reminding Judas, as well as the others, of a rabbinic teaching: although almsgiving and other works of justice were considered essential, the works of mercy, of which burial was one example, had primacy and were seen to be more perfect.

Jesus was aware that the disciples whom he loved would soon be subjected to the radical poverty of the loss of his physical presence. He recalled the teaching, not to emphasize the inevitability of social poverty, but to give voice to his keen awareness of the timeliness of Mary's extravagant offering of love toward him.

Through Mary's action of love we are privileged to see more clearly the power of Jesus' love and what our response of honor and worship of him can be. Her abandonment in love to Jesus, who passed through death and burial to glory, bears witness that only love is strong enough to transcend death (Song of Songs 8:6).

Within us, the spirit of Mary of Bethany is present to prompt and encourage our hearts to grasp the moment, to "follow Christ by loving as he loved . . . giving himself . . . as a fragrant offering . . ." (Eph. 5:2).

Suggested Approach to Prayer: The Fragrance of Presence

+ *Daily prayer pattern:* (See pages 1 and 2.)
I quiet myself and relax in the presence of God.
I declare my dependency on God.

+ *Grace:* I ask to know and love Jesus more intimately so that I may follow him in faith and with courage.

+ *Method:* Contemplation, as on page 3 and Centering, as on page 4.
I image myself at the table in Bethany. I consider the joy present among the friends who gather with Jesus. I am also aware of undercurrents of sadness and a feeling of dread.

I look at each face around the table. I take note of what I see and feel.

I watch Mary. I become aware of what her face reveals of her inner spirit as she strokes the feet of Jesus with the perfumed ointment. I allow the fragrance to gently enfold me.

I image the fragrance as the presence of Jesus. Slowly and deeply, I breathe in this fragrance of the presence of Jesus. I allow this presence to permeate my entire being . . . every cell of my body to be filled with his essence.

Within the recesses of myself, I periodically repeat the prayer, "Glory and honor to you, Lord Jesus Christ."

I contemplate the face of Jesus. I see, behind his eyes, knowledge of the deeper meaning of this moment. I am *with* him.

Can I find it in my heart to kneel at the feet of Jesus, and with Mary, to anoint his feet?

+ *Closing:* I allow my heart to speak intimately and deeply to the heart of Christ.

I pray the Our Father.

+ *Review of Prayer:* In my journal, I record the thoughts and feelings that surfaced during the time of prayer.

Week 1, Day 6: Repetition

Suggested Approach to Prayer

+ *Daily prayer pattern:* (See pages 1 and 2.)
I quiet myself and relax in the presence of God.
I declare my dependency on God.

+ *Grace:* I ask God to allow me to enter into sorrow as I stay with Christ in his sufferings borne on my behalf and because of my sins.

+ *Method:* Repetition, as on page 6.
In preparation, I review my prayer periods by reading my journal of the past week. I select for my repetition the period of prayer in which I was most deeply moved, or one in which I experienced a lack of emotional response, or one in which I was grasped with insight, or one in which I experienced confusion. I use the method with which I approached the passage initially. I open myself to hear again God's word to me in that particular passage.

+ *Review of Prayer:* I write in my journal any feelings, experiences, or insights that have surfaced in this "second listening."

if anyone wants
to be a follower
of mine,
let him...
take up his cross
every day....
Luke 9:23

Week 2, Day 1: He Who Comes

MATTHEW 21:1–17

When they were near Jerusalem and had come in sight of Bethphage on the Mount of Olives, Jesus sent two disciples, • saying to them, "Go to the village facing you, and you will immediately find a tethered donkey and a colt with her. Untie them and bring them to me. • If anyone says anything to you, you are to say, 'The Master needs them and will send them back directly.'" • This took place to fulfill the prophecy:

> Say to the daughter of Zion:
> Look, your king comes to you;
> he is humble, he rides on a donkey
> and on a colt, the foal of a beast of burden.

• So the disciples went out and did as Jesus had told them. • They brought the donkey and the colt, then they laid their cloaks on their backs and he sat on them. • Great crowds of people spread their cloaks on the road, while others were cutting branches from the trees and spreading them in his path. • The crowds who went in front of him and those who followed were all shouting:

> "Hosanna to the Son of David!
> Blessings on him who comes in the name of the Lord!
> Hosanna in the highest heavens!"

And when he entered Jerusalem, the whole city was in turmoil. "Who is this?" people asked, • and the crowds answered, "This is the prophet Jesus from Nazareth in Galilee."

Jesus then went into the Temple and drove out all those who were selling and buying there; he upset the tables of the money changers and the chairs of those who were selling pigeons. • "According to scripture" he said, "my house will be called a house of prayer; *but you are turning it into a rob-ber's den." • There were also blind and lame people who came to him in the Temple, and he cured them. • At the sight of the wonderful things he did and of the children shouting, "Hosanna to the Son of David" in the Temple, the chief priests and the scribes were indignant. • "Do you hear what they are saying?" they said to him. "Yes," Jesus answered "have you never read this:*

> By the mouths of children, babes in arms,
> you have made sure of praise?"

• *With that he left them and went out of the city to Bethany where he spent the night.*

What would become of us if we did not hope, if we did not nurture hope, if we did not risk believing in the unexpected and the unseen?

Christ Jesus *is* our hope (1 Tim. 1:1)!

On the occasion of his dramatic entry into the city of Jerusalem, Jesus was seen and celebrated as the fulfillment of the hope that had shaped centuries of longing and expectation.

His entry was a highly charged symbolic drama. Jesus, himself, set the stage. It was he who chose to make his ascent into the city from the Mount of Olives, a place long identified with messianic hope (Zech. 14:4). By deliberately choosing to enter the city riding on a donkey, long associated with kings in peaceful times, Jesus laid claim to being a king of peace.

All the aspects of his entrance into Jerusalem revealed Jesus' radical claim to be Son of David, the hoped-for Messiah. An unmistakable note of majesty and kingship accompanied Jesus' progress through the city toward the Temple where he would assert his liberating authority as God's Son.

The people were exuberant in response, spreading cloaks and branches in his path. Indeed, they welcomed him royally, shouting, "Hosanna!" The sight of Jesus and the significance of the event so exhilarated the people that the entire city of Jerusalem seemed shaken to its very foundation.

Jesus accepted their recognition and homage. For the first time, on the threshold of his passion, he allowed the people to claim him as their Messiah. Once again, he had extended himself in love, offering to them a challenging invitation to open their hearts to him. They recognized, accepted, and heralded him as the one "who comes in the name of the Lord."

Jesus came humbly, a coming that contrasted sharply with the messianic expectations of the time. His arena was not the palaces of diplomacy where political alliances were forged, nor was it the battlefield where military victory was sought at any cost. No, Jesus moved among the people, among the blind and the despairing, offering hope to the lame and the crippled in body and spirit. His stance was one of humility, the humility of authenticity, a humility born of inner strength.

On the day of his entrance into Jerusalem, Jesus, the people's Messiah, revealed a fearless and uncompromising strength as he proceeded directly to the center of the city, into the sanctuary, reclaiming and restoring the Temple as the house of God.

The marvelous procession into Jerusalem and the manifestation of the healing, restoring power of Jesus foreshadowed the fullness of time when Jesus would return in glory.

This occasion, like that of the transfiguration, filled the early Christians with hope and sustained them in their hour of darkness.

We, as contemporary Christians, are part of the great procession of those who have followed Jesus. Filled with his Spirit, we become a sign of hope for others. In oneness with Jesus we bring his healing presence to an anguished world, a world broken and yearning for wholeness.

Suggested Approach to Prayer: The Man on the Donkey

+ *Daily prayer pattern:* (See pages 1 and 2.)
  I quiet myself and relax in the presence of God.
  I declare my dependency on God.

+ *Grace:* I ask to know and love Jesus more intimately so that I may follow him in faith and with courage.

+ *Method:* Contemplation, as on page 3.

I image myself in the crowd on a narrow street in Jerusalem. I image in great detail the sights, sounds, and smells of the busy, over-crowded city.

I hear the excitement of the people as a procession approaches. I am aware of the jostling of the people around me as they strain to catch a glimpse of the man on the donkey.

I listen as I hear him acclaimed the Son of David, one who "comes in the name of the Lord."

I am aware of my feeling response as I see him approach, my excitement . . . confusion . . . fear . . . longing . . . hope . . . doubt . . . expectation . . .

I image my own reaction. Do I join the following, or do I withdraw? I am aware of my feelings as I enter or do not enter into the procession.

As Jesus passes, I focus on his face and pay particular attention to his expression and what meaning it reveals of this moment for him.

I hear someone shout, "Who is this?" I let my heart respond.

+ *Closing:* I ask Mary to intercede for me that I would receive the gift of total dependency on God. I ask that I would be so detached from all things that I would put all my talents, possessions, and achievements at the service of Christ. I pray to follow in the pattern of Christ's life—even to the end. Providing it would not be sinful on anyone's part, I pray that if it is God's wish for me, I would have, like Christ, the courage and strength to endure poverty and/or personal humiliation.

I pray the Hail Mary.

In the company of Mary, I approach Jesus and offer the same prayer, that he would obtain these graces for me from my Creator. I pray "Soul of Christ," p. 138.

In the presence of Jesus and Mary, and offered by them, I approach God my Creator. Again I make the same request.

I pray the Our Father.

+ *Review of Prayer:* I write in my journal what has surfaced in my prayer as a call to my closer following of Jesus, attending especially to the feelings that were present.

Week 2, Day 2: Harvest Yield

JOHN 12:23–32

Jesus replied to them:

> *"Now the hour has come*
> *for the Son of Man to be glorified.*
> *I tell you, most solemnly,*
> *Unless a wheat grain falls on the ground and dies,*
> *it remains only a single grain;*
> *but if it dies,*
> *it yields a rich harvest.*
> *Anyone who loves his life loses it;*
> *anyone who hates his life in this world*
> *will keep it for the eternal life.*
> *If [anyone] serves me, he must follow me,*
> *wherever I am, my servant will be there too.*
> *If anyone serves me, my Father will honour him.*
> *Now my soul is troubled.*
> *What shall I say:*
> *Father, save me from this hour?*
> *But it was for this very reason that I have come to this*
> *   hour.*
> *Father, glorify your name!"*

A voice came from heaven, "I have glorified it, and I will glorify it again."

People standing by, who heard this, said it was a clap of thunder; others said, "It was an angel speaking to him." • Jesus answered, "It was not for my sake that this voice came, but for yours.

> *"Now sentence is being passed on this world;*
> *now the prince of this world is to be overthrown.*
> *And when I am lifted up from the earth,*
> *I shall draw all people to myself."*

38

The "hour" of Jesus is our *present* hour. The hour is not an hour of death, but an hour of birth.

Jesus drew on the fecundity of nature to illustrate his hour and to exemplify his glorification, the harvest of life that his death would yield.

The imagery of the seed yielding to harvest awakens in us the rich experience and splendor of nature's fruitfulness.

> In perpetual transformation, the humble "rotting" seed lengthens into stock and sprouting leaves, long stem grows into dense bud, whence the blossom bursts forth in all its diversity into the green and gold of leaves and thence into the radiant color of the flower, culminates into the reversal by which the scented fragility of the blossom becomes the concentrated mature fruit, again with its infinite variety of form, color, consistency, taste and smell (55, p. 51).

Jesus is the prototype of the self-life-givingness of those who believe. ". . . like a root out of dry ground. . . . he was despised and rejected . . . wounded for our transgressions . . . oppressed . . . afflicted. He was cut off out of the land of the living" (Isa. 53:2–3,5,7–8, RSV).

The Greek Gentiles, to whom Jesus replied in this passage from John, are the prototype of the mature fruit which issued forth through Jesus' offering of self. ". . . he shall see his off-spring. . . . he shall see the fruit of the travail of his soul and be satisfied . . ." (Isa. 53:10–11, RSV).

The presence of the Gentiles symbolizes the universality of the Christian community, which embraces all diversities in its fold. The occasion of the Gentiles coming to Jesus signaled for him the arrival of his hour. The time for reconciliation had come. All would be drawn together in him through the outpouring of himself in love.

A people newly formed through his death and resurrection announced a new era.

This birthing of a community was not without labor and suffering. Jesus was fearful and struggled with the temptation to ask the Father to spare him. Yet, trusting in God's love, he surrendered, letting go his fear of death, his clinging to life.

Jesus' submission is the model for our own. In the bringing forth of new life, he was unable to escape death. His followers, too, will be faced throughout their lives with choosing death to selfishness as the only true path to life. Therefore, love for life means "hating" one's life, that is, hating within one's life any self-seeking that serves as an obstacle to loving. "In the evening of life," said St. John of the Cross, "we will be judged by love."

The voice of the Father affirms Jesus' selfless prayer, "Father, glorify your name." Once again, as in the transfiguration, God's glory became visible. God reassured Jesus, and Jesus is, in turn, our reassurance. His death is the culminating triumph of God's evolving plan for creation. All things created are being drawn into oneness with Jesus and carried in his spirit into eternal life which, present even now, continues to burst forth in a "rich harvest."

Suggested Approach to Prayer: My Tree

+ *Daily prayer pattern:* (See pages 1 and 2.)
  I quiet myself and relax in the presence of God.
  I declare my dependency on God.

+ *Grace:* I ask to know and love Jesus more intimately so that I may follow him more closely in faith and with courage.

+ *Method:* Contemplation, as on page 3.
  I image myself returning to the place of my birth. I consider what the weather is like on my birth day, for example, sunny, overcast . . . I see the fruit tree, the seed of which I image was planted by my parents on the day of my birth.

  I consider where my tree was planted, perhaps in the corner of the yard, in an open field, one of many in an orchard . . .

  I am aware of my feelings as I see my tree for the first time in many years. For example, I might feel excitement, disappointment, or surprise as I see how tall it is, how full it is, whether it is straight or crooked.

  I circle around my tree, viewing it from different angles, seeing the spread of its branches, the color of its foliage. I approach it and touch the bark, and I am aware of how it feels, whether it feels smooth, irregular, coarse.

I consider the fruit hanging from the branches—whether it is abundant or skimpy or barren. I take careful note of the quality of the fruit, its color, its fragrance. I pick a fruit, feel its contours, taste of it.

I consider how I feel about my tree, what I like or do not like about it. I speak to my tree, and I hear it respond to me.

I become the tree. I consider how it feels to be my tree, to own as my own its stature, its character, and its fruit.

I see Jesus approach. I consider how he looks at me, what he says to me, whether or not he takes a fruit from my branches. He speaks to me of my fruit, and I respond. I continue to listen to and speak with Jesus.

After the dialogue with Jesus, I become my self. As I prepare to leave, I look reverently at my tree, prayerfully considering how all I am was present in the promise of its seed. I consider if and how my tree and its fruit have changed since I arrived. I become aware of how my feelings about my tree and the seeds of its fruitfulness have changed.

+ *Closing:* I ask Mary to intercede for me that I would receive the gift of total dependency on God. I ask that I would be so detached from all things that I would put all my talents, possessions, and achievements at the service of Christ. I pray to follow in the pattern of Christ's life—even to the end. Providing it would not be sinful on anyone's part, I pray that if it is God's wish for me, I would have, like Christ, the courage and strength to endure poverty and/or personal humiliation.

I pray the Hail Mary.

In the company of Mary, I approach Jesus and offer the same prayer, that he would obtain these graces for me from my Creator. I pray "Soul of Christ," p. 138.

In the presence of Jesus and Mary, and offered by them, I approach God my Creator. Again I make the same request.

I pray the Our Father.

+ *Review of Prayer:* I write in my journal what has surfaced in my prayer, attending especially to the feelings that were present.

Week 2, Day 3:
A Basin, Some Water, and a Towel

JOHN 13:1–16

It was before the festival of the Passover, and Jesus knew that the hour had come for him to pass from this world to the Father. He had always loved those who were his in the world, but now he showed how perfect his love was.

They were at supper, and the devil had already put it into the mind of Judas Iscariot son of Simon, to betray him. • Jesus knew that the Father had put everything into his hands, and that he had come from God and was returning to God, • and he got up from table, removed his outer garment and, taking a towel, wrapped it round his waist; • he then poured water into a basin and began to wash the disciples' feet and to wipe them with the towel he was wearing.

He came to Simon Peter, who said to him, "Lord, are you going to wash my feet?" • Jesus answered, "At the moment you do not know what I am doing, but later you will understand." • "Never!" said Peter "You shall never wash my feet." Jesus replied, "If I do not wash you, you can have nothing in common with me." • "Then, Lord," said Simon Peter "not only my feet, but my hands and my head as well!" • Jesus said, "No one who has taken a bath needs washing, he is clean all over. You too are clean, though not all of you are." • He knew who was going to betray him, that was why he said, "though not all of you are."

When he had washed their feet and put on his clothes again he went back to the table. "Do you understand" he said "what I have done to you? • You call me Master and Lord, and rightly; so I am. • If I, then, the Lord and Master, have washed your feet, you should wash each other's feet. • I have

*given you an example so that you may copy what I have
done to you.*

*"I tell you most solemnly,
no servant is greater than his master,
no messenger is greater than the [one] who sent him."*

A basin, some water, and a towel—ordinary means to serve an extraordinary love!

Jesus' extravagant love for his disciples motivated the gentle and humble act of washing their feet. This deliberate action by Jesus also spoke of the profound level of awareness he had of his impending death.

Just as Mary's anointing of Jesus' feet foretold of his future embalmment, washing the disciples' feet symbolized his approaching death—the ultimate act of his love—which would cleanse and heal them of their sinfulness and ensure their heritage in him.

This incident is one of the most tender in the Gospels. Washing his disciples' feet was for Jesus, and for them, an intimate moment of transparent vulnerability and surrender. Not even the evil intent active within Judas could destroy its spirit of goodness.

This simple, human gesture not only gave expression to the love which had grown between Jesus and his disciples throughout the years of the public ministry, but also represented the disciples' initiation into their own mature ministry without their master's physical presence.

"I have given you an example so that you may copy what I have done to you."

As Jesus laid down his garments, he was deeply conscious of the nearness of the hour in which he would lay down his life for those he loved. Wrapping a towel around his waist in the manner of a slave, he, the master and Lord, voluntarily submitted himself to the radicalness of a love that serves. In this reversal of roles, Jesus called his disciples, also, to become willing servants of love, even to the point of laying down *their* lives for others (John 15:13).

The water Jesus poured over their feet was the cleansing water of purification, a symbol of his self-emptying death. So wonderful was his act of love that

Peter and the others would be able to comprehend the full import of it only after Jesus' death and resurrection. Only then, would they understand the baptismal symbolism of their experience.

In their newly created community they would experience the joy of oneness with the Risen Christ and grasp the full significance of baptism in the Spirit.

A basin, some water, and a towel had become for the disciples, and for us, a powerful prophetic symbol of the wholeness of Jesus' life, death, resurrection, and ascension—the wholeness of his love.

Suggested Approach to Prayer: Bathed in Love

+ *Daily prayer pattern:* (See pages 1 and 2.)
I quiet myself and relax in the presence of God.
I declare my dependency on God.

+ *Grace:* I ask to know and love Jesus more intimately so that I may follow him more closely in faith and with courage.

+ *Method:* Contemplation, as on page 3.
I image Jesus walking into our church on a Sunday morning. I see him open his hands to us and say, in a way that speaks to our hearts, "I have not called you servants, but friends."

I am aware of what passes through my mind, what surges in my heart, as I hear him say these words.

I see Jesus look over the gathered assembly. He calls forth a number of people. I hear him call the names of several others, and I see their response, how they rise reluctantly or eagerly . . .

I hear him call my name and see him look at me lovingly and humbly. I take care to experience within me both these attitudes of Christ as he looks at me.

I see Jesus gather those he has specially called. He invites us to be seated in the sanctuary. Then, deliberately and lovingly, he brings a basin of water and some towels. He disrobes and stands before us, stripped except for a loin cloth. I notice the shadow of scars on his side . . . his hands . . . his feet.

Jesus kneels before me and begins to wash my feet. I am acutely aware of

44

my feelings, perhaps of embarrassment . . . or wonder and awe . . . tenderness . . .

When Jesus has finished, he says to me, "As I have done for you, go and do likewise for the others."

I consider: To whom will I go? How will the intimacy and love of Jesus for me spill over into my family? into my faith community? to others?

+ *Closing:* (Review the Colloquy section on page 10.)

I conclude my prayer with a heartfelt conversation with Christ. I let it be a prayer of personal friendship, expressing my hopes, my needs, and my praise, thanks, and love.

I pray the Our Father.

+ *Review of Prayer:* I write in my journal the feelings and insights that have surfaced during my prayer.

Week 2, Day 4: In Remembrance

LUKE 22:14–23

When the hour came he took his place at table, and the apostles with him. • And he said to them, "I have longed to eat this passover with you before I suffer; • because, I tell you, I shall not eat it again until it is fulfilled in the kingdom of God."

Then, taking a cup, he gave thanks and said, "Take this and share it among you, • because from now on, I tell you, I shall not drink wine until the kingdom of God comes."

Then he took some bread, and when he had given thanks, broke it and gave it to them, saying, "This is my body which will be given for you; do this as a memorial of me." • He did the same with the cup after supper, and said, "This cup is the new covenant in my blood which will be poured out for you.

"And yet, here with me on the table is the hand of the man who betrays me. • The Son of Man does indeed go to his fate even as it has been decreed, but alas for that man by whom he is betrayed!" • And they began to ask one another which of them it could be who was to do this thing.

Our God is a God who remembers. In Jesus, God lives out his remembering.

On the evening before his death, Jesus shared a meal with his disciples. This last supper was a celebration of joyful remembrance, thanksgiving, and promise. Together they celebrated God's faithfulness to them throughout their history. They remembered how God had led them, never abandoned them, always been present.

This last meal, colored as it was by grief at Jesus' approaching death and impending betrayal, was, nevertheless, redolent with the promise Jesus made to them.

46

Jesus promised never to leave them, but to be present to them in a new, even fuller way. This shared meal initiated the disciples into a new relationship with Jesus, a relatonship of mutuality, in which they, too, had a commitment. It was to be a bond of loving friendship transcending death (Song of Songs 8:6).

The celebration took place within the context of the Passover festival, which was celebrated annually by the Jewish people. Passover recalled and relived the pivotal experience in their history when God delivered them out of Egyptian slavery (Exod. 12:1–14).

It was a festival of praise and elaborate ritual. Recalling the Exodus, the rite began with a preliminary blessing and cup of wine. Bitter herbs were then served to recall the bitterness of their suffering in Egypt. At this point in the meal, the youngest male child would ask, "What does this night mean?" His father would respond by telling the story of God's faithfulness to the people of God, thereby creating for future memory the image of a loving God who remembers.

After singing psalms and drinking a second cup of wine, new unleavened bread was blessed. It was eaten with the roasted Passover lamb. The blessing and drinking of a third cup of wine brought the meal to a close. The ritual remembrance was concluded with the singing of psalms of praise, "Blessings on him who comes in the name of Yahweh" (Ps. 118:26).

In Jesus, God lives out this remembrance—this everlasting faithfulness and loving kindness. In Jesus' life, the history of God's people, Israel, is recapitulated (Ps. 136).

At the last supper, Jesus reinterpreted and brought to greater fullness the symbols of the paschal ritual, interpreting the symbols in terms of himself. Jesus took the first cup and proclaimed the coming of the Kingdom when he would drink wine with them again.

He identified the unleavened bread with his own body. No longer to be known as the bread of affliction eaten in bondage, this bread was to be the bread of freedom. Through this bread, the disciples would experience the liberating presence of Christ with them, individually and communally.

Jesus identified the third cup of the paschal meal with the new covenant in his blood (Jer. 31:31–32). The sacrifice of the Passover lamb had given way to Jesus' offering of his own self, the offering of his entire life, culminating now in his death. Because blood is life (Lev. 17:11) and the flow of blood unites in one life, Jesus' blood symbolizes and effects a forceful union between God and the people of God. Jesus' covenant of blood is a covenant of life.

"Do this in memory of me." Jesus told his disciples to continue living their relationship of love with him through the continuing celebration of his presence among them. He promised that in their future remembering, in the memorializing of his presence, he would re-present himself to the Christian community whenever they, recalling his last shared meal with them, blessed and shared bread and wine.

In this living re-presentation of himself, in love, for them, they would experience their union with him and with each other. Through their active participation in this memorial celebration they would be incorporated in the power of Jesus' death and resurrection, and their lives, like his, would be blessed and given for others.

"Do this in memory of me." In bread broken and wine poured, we receive our lives, the healing of what has been, the joy of who we truly are, the promise of all we may yet be.

Suggested Approach to Prayer: At the Table

+ *Daily prayer pattern:* (See pages 1 and 2.)
I quiet myself and relax in the presence of God.
I declare my dependency on God.

+ *Grace:* I ask to know and love Jesus more intimately and that I may enter into sorrow as I stay with Christ in his suffering.

+ *Method:* Contemplation, as on page 3.
I image myself at the table with Jesus and his disciples. I see the room in which all are gathered and notice if it is big or small, well lit or dark, warm or chilly . . .
I see the table, its cloth, the cups and other dishes . . .
I observe the disciples as they recline at table, allowing myself time to take note of each individual's expression, whether he appears to be joyous, fearful, expectant, sad . . .

I listen attentively to their words, particularly to the way the words are spoken, whether they connote love, kindness, grief, fear, deceit . . .

Aware of Jesus' approaching death, I focus my attention on him. I see his expression, the way he looks at his disciples. I allow myself to contemplate his face. I am particularly aware of feelings I experience when I look into his face.

I hear Jesus speak. I listen as he leads his followers through the Passover ritual. I watch and listen as he blesses and shares bread and wine with them, and invites them to do this in memory of him. I am attentive to my feelings, for example, of awe, confusion, blessing, feeling included or left out . . .

I ask Jesus, "What does this night mean?" I allow myself to be quietly present as I receive Jesus' response within me.

+ *Closing:* I ask Mary to intercede for me that I would receive the gift of total dependency on God. I ask that I would be so detached from all things that I would put all my talents, possessions, and achievements at the service of Christ. I pray to follow in the pattern of Christ's life—even to the end. Providing it would not be sinful on anyone's part, I pray that if it is God's wish for me, I would have, like Christ, the courage and strength to endure poverty and/or personal humiliation.

I pray the Hail Mary.

In the company of Mary, I approach Jesus and offer the same prayer, that he would obtain these graces for me from my Creator. I pray "Soul of Christ," p. 138.

In the presence of Jesus and Mary, and offered by them, I approach God my Creator. Again I make the same request.

I pray the Our Father.

+ *Review of Prayer:* I write in my journal what has surfaced in my prayer as a call to my closer following of Jesus, attending especially to the feelings that were present.

Week 2, Day 5:
The Secret Place; The Sacred Place

JOHN 17:1–26

After saying this, Jesus raised his eyes to heaven and said:

"Father, the hour has come:
glorify your Son
so that your Son may glorify you;
and, through the power over all [people] that you
        have given him,
let him give eternal life to all those you have entrusted
        to him.
And eternal life is this:
to know you,
the only true God,
and Jesus Christ whom you have sent.
I have glorified you on earth
and finished the work
that you gave me to do.
Now, Father, it is time for you to glorify me
with that glory I had with you
before ever the world was.
I have made your name known
to [those] you took from the world to give me.
They were yours and you gave them to me,
and they have kept your word.
Now at last they know
that all you have given me comes indeed from you;
for I have given them
the teaching you gave to me,
and they have truly accepted this, that I came from you,
and have believed that it was you who sent me.
I pray for them;
I am not praying for the world

but for those you have given me,
because they belong to you:
all I have is yours
and all you have is mine,
and in them I am glorified.
I am not in the world any longer,
but they are in the world,
and I am coming to you.
Holy Father,
keep those you have given me true to your name,
so that they may be one like us.
While I was with them,
I kept those you had given me true to your name.
I have watched over them and not one is lost
except the one who chose to be lost,
and this was to fulfill the scriptures.
But now I am coming to you
and while still in the world I say these things
to share my joy with them to the full.
I passed your word on to them,
and the world hated them,
because they belong to the world
no more than I belong to the world.
I am not asking you to remove them from the world,
but to protect them from the evil one.
They do not belong to the world
any more than I belong to the world.
Consecrate them in the truth;
your word is truth.
As you sent me into the world,
I have sent them into the world,
and for their sake I consecrate myself
so that they too may be consecrated in truth.
I pray not only for these,

51

but for those also
who through their words will believe in me.
May they all be one.
Father, may they be one in us,
as you are in me and I am in you,
so that the world may believe it was you who sent me.

I have given them the glory you gave to me,
that they may be one as we are one.
With me in them and you in me,
may they be so completely one
that the world will realize that it was you who sent me
and that I have loved them as much as you loved me.
Father,
I want those you have given me
to be with me where I am,
so that they may always see the glory
you have given me
because you loved me
before the foundation of the world.
Father, Righteous One,
the world has not known you,
but I have known you,
and these have known
that you have sent me.
I have made your name known to them
and will continue to make it known,
so that the love with which you loved me may be in
them,
and so that I may be in them."

"Father, the hour has come:
glorify your son
so that your son may glorify you."

Abba, loving and gracious God
    You have been with me always
    You are with me now as I am about to die.

            Hear my prayer
            Remember your promise.

I pray
    that your goodness will be revealed
                        in my life
                        and
                        in my dying.

            Remember your promise, O God.

I pray
    not for myself
I pray
    for all those I love
I pray
    that my death will be for them
            a new beginning. . .
                    a beginning
                        of seeing and knowing you
                    an entry
                        into love with you,
                        a love unique . . .

"I pray for them."

Abba, near and compassionate God

    As I am about to leave them,
    I hold in my heart those I most love.

    I have planted your name in their hearts.
            Your word dwells there.

Be with them.
Comfort them.
Protect them.

Lead them into healing.
Guide them in truth.

Gift them, Lord God, with the joy of being in your presence.

"May they all be one."

Abba, God of the future, God of hope.

I place before you all of creation
        those born
            and
        those to be born.

I celebrate
        dreams not yet dreamed
        hopes expected, yet unseen

I am filled with utter confidence—
    I trust in your promise.
    You have given me
        a glimpse of yourself
        shining
        in the love

                of those who believe
                of those who have found

the secret place   the sacred space

of
oneness
in
YOU

Suggested Approach to Prayer: The Mind and Heart of Jesus

+ *Daily prayer pattern:* (See pages 1 and 2.)
I quiet myself and relax in the presence of God.
I declare my dependency on God.

+ *Grace:* I ask to know and love Jesus more intimately so that I share in his mind and heart as he enters into the passion.

+ *Method:* Meditative Reading, as on page 5.
I image Jesus at prayer. I enter into the mind and heart of Jesus on the night before he died.
I allow myself to taste of his love and his concern, of his prayer for those he loved.
I slowly read John 17:1–26. I pause periodically to allow the words and phrases to resonate within the realm of my own experience.
I respond to Christ and his love for me.
I am aware of my feeling response, that of gratitude, awe, amazement . . .

+ *Closing:* (Review the Colloquy section on page 10.)
I let my heart speak to Christ.
I close with an Our Father.

+ *Review of Prayer:* In my journal, I record my own prayer response to Jesus' prayer.

Week 2, Day 6: Repetition

Suggested Approach to Prayer:

+ *Daily prayer pattern:* (See pages 1 and 2.)
I quiet myself and relax in the presence of God.
I declare my dependency on God.

+ *Grace:* I ask God to allow me to enter into sorrow as I stay with Christ in his suffering, borne on my behalf and because of my sins.

+ *Method:* Repetition, as on page 6.
In preparation, I review my prayer periods since the last repetition day. I select for my repetition the period of prayer in which I was most deeply moved or the one in which I experienced a lack of emotional response, or one in which I was grasped with insight or experienced confusion. I use the method with which I approached the passage initially. I open myself to hear again God's word to me in that particular passage.

+ *Review of Prayer:* I write in my journal any feelings, experiences, or insights that have surfaced in this "second listening."

Week 3, Day 1: Out of the Darkness

MARK 14:32–42

They came to a small estate called Gethsemane, and Jesus said to his disciples, "Stay here while I pray." • Then he took Peter and James and John with him. And a sudden fear came over him, and great distress. • And he said to them, "My soul is sorrowful to the point of death. Wait here, and keep awake." • And going on a little further he threw himself on the ground and prayed that, if it were possible, this hour might pass him by. • "Abba (Father)!" he said "Everything is possible for you. Take this cup away from me. But let it be as you, not I, would have it." • He came back and found them sleeping, and he said to Peter, "Simon, are you asleep? Had you not the strength to keep awake one hour? • You should be awake, and praying not to be put to the test. The spirit is willing, but the flesh is weak." • Again he went away and prayed, saying the same words. • And once more he came back and found them sleeping, their eyes were so heavy; and they could find no answer for him. • He came back a third time and said to them, "You can sleep on now and take your rest. It is all over. The hour has come. Now the Son of Man is to be betrayed into the hands of sinners. • Get up! Let us go! My betrayer is close at hand already."

Your presence, Father . . . I approach.
I have very little time, as you well know.
Do you recognize my voice?
Must I reintroduce myself? . . .
You surely remember, Father? . . .
Always you have heard *my* voice,
Always you have saluted me
with a rainbow, a raven, a plague, something.

58

But now I see nothing. This time
you show me
Nothing at all. . . .

(12, part 2)

This anguished prayer might have been Jesus' own as he enters into his agony.

Through the use of the *kaddish*, the profound Jewish prayer for the dead, Leonard Bernstein has given poetic, as well as musical, expression to the universal, human experience of suffering and surrender. His composition touches a chord of resonance in every human heart.

Can Jesus, whose entire life had been an experience of God's loving presence, now, in the garden of Gethsemane, be crying out for mere recognition?

Can Jesus, whose life, whose every word and action, mirrored his intimate union with God, possibly be experiencing such *god-forsakenness?*

The horror and pain, the confusion, alienation, and deadly anxiety that Jesus experienced in the garden is nearly indescribable. The abyss of human aloneness and fear has always eluded adequate expression, yet ironically this very experience of intimate and intense suffering serves as the caldron of heroism and creativity. One can only imagine the sincerity and love with which Mark sought to convey the suffering of Jesus.

The struggle, throughout the ages, to give expression to the profoundly human experience of self-acceptance and surrender has shaped and inspired generations.

The prayer that is forming in the heart of Christ as he descends from the upper room and passes through the city gate to the garden is the prayer of one who is being thrust down into nothingness. In the bleakness of this void, Jesus must grapple with the ultimate meaning of life.

In facing death, Jesus encounters the finality of life's distortion—sin, the alienation from God.

His boundless love for humankind and solidarity with all creation makes Jesus totally open and vulnerable, and this very openness of loving exposes him to the crushing weight of sin (Isa. 53:10). Only Jesus, who experiences the ultimate nearness to God, can fully grasp the absurd tragedy and horror of sin. So great is his awareness of the world's loss that, overwhelmed by love, he literally experiences the loneliness and forsakenness of his loss (Isa. 53:4). Crushed and powerless, almost despairing, Jesus cries out into the dark void, one word, "Abba."

He who came from heaven presses himself into the sin-scarred earth, seeking protection in a hole where only death is master (64, p. 223).

"Abba"—the primal cry resounding against the impenetrable darkness of sin.

"Abba"—the unanswerable plea for mercy and relief.

"Abba"—the last desperate cry that precedes the capitulation of total weakness, making way for God's grace of surrender.

The surrender of Jesus to God stands in sharp contrast to the response of the disciples. He dares to enter the darkness; they sleep through the night. Yet, his acceptance reconciles their denials (Isa. 53:11).

Through Jesus' total surrender, God's plan for Jesus is brought to fulfillment.

The absolute emptiness of Jesus invites the absolute gift of God's grace. Nothing changes. Jesus will be "handed over" to death. Everything changes! Filled with God's strength, Jesus rises to face his betrayer, "Get up, let us go."

Suggested Approach to Prayer: Into the Garden

+ *Daily prayer pattern:* (See pages 1 and 2.)
I quiet myself and relax in the presence of God.
I declare my dependency on God.

+ *Grace:* I ask to share in the agony, to feel sorrow with Christ in sorrow, to be anguished with Christ's anguish, even to experience tears because of Christ's love for me.

+ *Method:* Contemplation, as on page 3.
In the company of Jesus, I leave the room of the supper. Slowly I descend the steps and walk through the city. I walk beside Jesus as he makes his entry through the gate into the garden.

In great detail, I image the physical surroundings that are part of our short journey: how dark it has become, how cold or warm the night air, the winding path, the presence of the trees, the sounds and scents of the night.

I take particular note of Jesus, of his facial expression and posture and what they reveal of his inner attitude.

I see Jesus as he withdraws into a private space of prayer. As I contemplate his deepening anguish, I ponder the depth of love that moves one to such profound sorrow.

I consider what it would be like and how I would respond if some one I loved were to be condemned for a serious crime, perhaps a friend . . . my spouse . . . my child . . .

I consider how their suffering, their shame and despair, their utter isolation would be my own. I consider how overwhelmingly poignant my pain would be, how helpless I would feel, how desperate my prayer . . .

Having considered my own vulnerability in loving, I move to consider the depth of pain Jesus must have endured as he dared to embrace the entire world in unlimited love, as he suffered the sinfulness, the condemnation, and alienation of those he loved.

+ *Closing:* (Review the Colloquy section on page 10.)

I speak with Jesus, sharing with him how my own human experience of loving gives me a glimpse into his deep compassion. I speak to him of my deep gratitude for his loving me, my loved ones, and the entire world with such a total self-giving love. I join with Jesus in offering his prayer of surrender, "Abba, not my will but yours be done."

I pray the Our Father.

+ *Review of Prayer:* I record in my journal the feelings and insights that surfaced during the hour of prayer.

Week 3, Day 2: Abba—Our Father

MATTHEW 6:9b–13

> *"Our Father in heaven,*
> *may your name be held holy,*
> *your kingdom come,*
> *your will be done,*
> *on earth as in heaven.*
>
> *Give us today our daily bread.*
> *And forgive us our debts,*
> *as we have forgiven those who are in debt to us.*
> *And do not put us to the test,*
> *but save us from the evil one."*

Our Father
    In the garden
        dark compost of human hunger
        chaotic womb of possibility
Births—in lightning and love—surrender!
        One moment, one time
            transparent grail
                of all time
                    every moment.
    Earth arching to meet her maker
    Energy leaping from pole to pole
        and all
            emerging
            converging
The Stillpoint, Son of Man and Son of God
        prays
                "Our Father"

The Lord's Prayer reflects the spirit in which Jesus lived his entire life. It is as if every daily moment of commitment, every hour of contemplation, every spontaneous turning to God somehow shaped this profound prayer of praise and petition. Not surprisingly, in the time of his greatest testing, in the Garden of Gethsemane, the words that rose from Jesus' heart echoed those of the Our Father.

By addressing God as "our Father," Jesus not only claimed his identity as God's Son, but acknowledged his solidarity with all women and men for all time. Because of Jesus and his love for us, we too can pray, "*our* Father" (Rom. 8:14–15).

The prayer has a sense of urgency, a "here, now, and soon" (20, 198); unfortunately, frequent and thoughtless repetition has dissipated some of its immediacy. Too many Christians have lost a sense of expectation for the Second Coming, the Parousia.

"Thy kingdom come."

The expected and hoped for kingdom is a time and a place, a here and a now, present yet always evolving. It is a movement forward in trust that magnetically charges and draws all human hearts.

Jesus prayed that this kingdom of love would be actualized in earthly history. He prayed that the name of God—father, mother, creator—would be cherished and thereby authentically shape the lives of his followers as sons and daughters of God.

Jesus' prayer that "God's will be done" urges us to enter into collaboration with God, to make a personal commitment of total dedication to do all we can, within our own situation and circumstances, to bring the goodness of God to full realization.

Like Jesus in Gethsemane, we pray for the fullness of the kingdom in the sufferings of the "not yet." In Jesus, we live expectantly in the knowledge of his risen presence. Yet, in these "in between" times, we are a people who wait. Jesus gives us a prayer to support us in our waiting.

Our prayer is for "food, forgiveness and freedom from evil" (52, 61).

We pray for bread, but not only for the bread of daily sustenance. We ask for and receive the eucharistic bread, which sustains us in the waiting and anticipates the banquet celebration of Omega.

We pray for forgiveness. We are a community bonded in unconditional love and reconciliation. As we receive and mediate God's gracious forgiveness, we participate in God's ongoing creation and healing of the world.

We pray for freedom from the power of sin, which the apocalyptic clash between goodness and evil unleashes. Trusting, we receive the strength and the courage to make the prayer of Jesus the reality of our own self-surrender.

Suggested Approach to Prayer: Our Father

+ *Daily prayer pattern:* (See pages 1 and 2.)
  I quiet myself and relax in the presence of God.
  I declare my dependency on God.

+ *Grace:* I ask to enter with Jesus into his prayer in the garden, to share his surrender to the Father.

+ *Method:* Meditative Reading, as on page 5.
  I enter into the garden with Jesus. I sit beside him and quietly begin to pray the Our Father.
  Beginning with the word "Father," I remain with each word of the prayer, gently repeating it for as long a time as it speaks to me, for as long as it touches me interiorly.
  I proceed this way throughout the text of the prayer.
  If any word or phrase seems particularly fruitful, I rest with its resonance, allowing myself to absorb the fullness of its direction and/or consolation.

+ *Closing:* (Review the Colloquy section on page 10.)
  I let my heart speak simply, openly to Jesus.
  I pray the Our Father.

+ *Review of Prayer:* I record in my journal whatever insights and feelings surfaced during my prayer.

Week 3, Day 3: The Kiss

MATTHEW 26:47–56

He was still speaking when Judas, one of the Twelve, appeared, and with him a large number of men armed with swords and clubs, sent by the chief priests and elders of the people. • Now the traitor had arranged a sign with them. "The one I kiss," he had said "he is the man. Take him in charge." • So he went straight up to Jesus and said, "Greetings, Rabbi," and kissed him. • Jesus said to him, "My friend, do what you are here for." Then they came forward, seized Jesus and took him in charge. • At that, one of the followers of Jesus grasped his sword and drew it; he struck out at the high priest's servant, and cut off his ear. • Jesus then said, "Put your sword back, for all who draw the sword will die by the sword. • Or do you think that I cannot appeal to my Father who would promptly send more than twelve legions of angels to my defence? • But then, how would the scriptures be fulfilled that say this is the way it must be?" • It was at this time that Jesus said to the crowds, "Am I brigand, that you had to set out to capture me with swords and clubs? I sat teaching in the Temple day after day and you never laid hands on me." • Now all this happened to fulfil the prophecies in scripture. Then all the disciples deserted him and ran away.

In the darkness, a kiss calls forth surrender and new life.

In the Garden of Eden, God breathed the breath of life into Adam and he became a living spirit (Gen. 2:7).

In the Garden of Gethsemane, the breath of a kiss initiates the surrender which released into the entire world the compassionate spirit of Jesus.

In the surrender of Jesus to God *all* history, *all* prophecy will find fulfillment.

Just as, in the beginning, God's creative spirit hovered over the chaos (Gen. 1:2), God's creative spirit is now present and active in the darkness, in the confusion and anguish of human sinfulness and betrayal.

Who gave this kiss to Jesus? It was one of his own, a disciple whom he taught and loved, a friend with whom he shared life. Only such a loved one could have the power and the authority to seize, to hold, and to identify him.

It was Judas Iscariot. Though little is actually known about Judas and his motivation, legend invests his character with a, perhaps unwarranted, definitive degree of evil.

Dante, for example, places Judas in the pit of hell, at the lowest level of degradation. Along with the traitors Brutus and Cassius, he depicts Judas dangling from one of the mouths of Satan (3, *Inferno*, canto 34, lines 60ff)!

Others, somewhat more benevolently, suggest that Judas, as a member of the Zealots, was disappointed in Jesus and, with a miscalculated hope of forcing Jesus to action, collaborated with the enemy.

The deeper truth does not lie in making Judas the personification of evil, nor in justifying his actions and thereby excusing him of responsibility. The human personality is too complex for such simplistic judgments.

We cannot underestimate, however, the significance of the person of Judas, his presence and action, at this juncture in Jesus', life. Moreover, Judas' character and actions mirror the potential for evil and betrayal that stalks our own inner darkness.

Judas' betrayal of Jesus brings us face to face with the dark side of our selves. Examining it challenges us to a greater awareness of how we betray our God, ourselves, and each other.

Judas' betrayal was not the only betrayal Jesus experienced that night in the garden. Peter, as well as each of the other disciples, shared in the denial and desertion of their friend and mentor. What a crushing disappointment for Jesus to once again encounter his followers' fear and lack of understanding. In the critical moment they failed to comprehend his life-giving destiny, failed to support his mission of nonresistant surrender (Isa. 50:5).

Jesus faced his ordeal in utter aloneness.

Yet there is no fatalism, no stoicism, and no hesitancy in his decision or his actions.

Jesus knew his God and he knew his destiny.

Jesus was firmly grounded in the prophetic word that had shaped his people, and it sustained his heart in this hour.

In the darkness of the garden, the kiss of Judas found Jesus in readiness.

Suggested Approach to Prayer: Night of Betrayal

+ *Daily prayer pattern:* (See pages 1 and 2.)
I quiet myself and relax in the presence of God.
I declare my dependency on God.

+ *Grace:* I ask God to allow me to enter into sorrow as I stay with Christ in his suffering, borne on my behalf.

+ *Method:* Contemplation, as on page 3.
I place myself in the garden of Gethsemane. I note the darkness in the garden. I am aware of the scents and sounds of the night . . .

I am aware of the disciples who are present in the garden, of their expression and their awareness of Jesus as he turns toward the gate.

I hear the noises of an approaching mob and see the light of their torches as they approach.

As they draw nearer, I see the crude weapons they are carrying.

At the head of the mob I see Judas. I watch as he approaches Jesus and kisses him.

I listen attentively to the exchange between Jesus and Judas. I become aware of my response as I listen and watch.

I see some of the soldiers come forward to arrest Jesus. In the confusion that follows, I see a disciple strike one of the high priest's servants with a sword. I listen as Jesus reprimands the disciple.

I take particular note of Jesus' facial expression and the tone of his voice during this episode.

I continue to listen to Jesus as he speaks to the crowd.

As Jesus is arrested and led away, I am aware of how alone he is, that all his disciples have fled.

With the disciples, I ponder, how have I betrayed Jesus?

+ *Closing:* (Review the Colloquy section on page 10.)
I speak to Jesus of my love and my gratitude for his love.
I close my prayer with the Our Father.

+ *Review of Prayer:* I record in my journal my feeling responses and any new insights that have surfaced during this period of prayer.

Week 3, Day 4: The Night Before

LUKE 22:54–65

They seized him then and led him away, and they took him to the high priest's house. Peter followed at a distance. • They had lit a fire in the middle of the courtyard and Peter sat down among them, • and as he was sitting there by the blaze a servant-girl saw him, peered at him, and said, "This person was with him too." • But he denied it. "Woman," he said "I do not know him." • Shortly afterwards someone else saw him and said, "You are another of them." But Peter replied, "I am not, my friend." • About an hour later another man insisted, saying, "This fellow was certainly with him. Why, he is a Galilean." "My friend," said Peter "I do not know what you are talking about." At that instant, while he was still speaking, the cock crew, • and the Lord turned and looked straight at Peter, and Peter remembered what the Lord had said to him, "Before the cock crows today, you will have disowned me three times." • And he went outside and wept bitterly.

Meanwhile the men who guarded Jesus were mocking and beating him. • They blindfolded him and questioned him. "Play the prophet" they said. "Who hit you then?" • And they continued heaping insults on him.

Jerusalem sleeps. Within the dark bowels of its night a restlessness of hatred, irrationality, and fear ignites and tests all those within the deceptive warmth of its blaze.

It is into this enemy territory, to the house of the high priest, that Jesus is taken. After subjecting Jesus to a preliminary and illegal hearing, the priests and elders turn him over to a band of underlings who are to guard him through the night until morning when he will be formally tried and convicted.

In the outer courtyard a fire has been lit. It provides both heat and light and draws all present into its circle.

The gathering does not reflect, however, a campfire congeniality. Rather, the atmosphere is one of vulgarity and feverish agitation. It is a night void of all propriety and restriction, a Mardi Gras before Ash Wednesday. The guards seize the opportunity of their happenstance authority over Jesus to vent their abhorrent humor in the primitive cruelty of mockery and abuse.

Jesus, the prophet, the one whose eyes have looked with penetrating love into the souls of men and women, is subjected to the humiliating blindfold game of "guess who."

Among those who mill around the fire is one who has known that look of love. That one is Peter, trusted disciple and close friend of Jesus.

Peter has followed Jesus to this place, unaware that here will be his own time of greatest testing. Passionate in his declarations to follow Christ even to death, Peter is not without courage (Luke 22:33)! It is, in fact, this confident courage which makes him vulnerable to his own limitations.

And he fails!

After three years of faithful companionship in the company of Jesus, three years of struggle and growth, Peter, in a fear-filled moment of weakness, denies his relationship with Jesus.

Peter denies Jesus, not once, but three times. He vows he does not even know Jesus, and he likewise denies any association with the other disciples. His betrayal is a callous repudiation of the one thing which had given his life its greatest meaning.

"And the Lord turned and looked straight at Peter."

Peter sees not anger, but heartbreak in Jesus' face.

And Peter "wept bitterly."

Recognition of his overconfidence and base guilt plunges Peter's heart into grief.

In the darkness Peter weeps bitterly, sustained only by memories of Jesus' prayer and promise (Luke 22:62).

The night is long. Outside, Peter, purified and forgiven, weeps.

Near the dying embers in the courtyard, Jesus waits.

He had said, "I have come to bring fire to the earth, and how I wish it were blazing already! • There is a baptism I must still receive, and how great is my distress till it is over" (Luke 12:49-50)!

It has begun.

Suggested Approach to Prayer: The Look of Jesus

+ *Daily prayer pattern:* (See pages 1 and 2.)
I quiet myself and relax in the presence of God.
I declare my dependency on God.

+ *Grace:* I ask God to allow me to enter into sorrow as I stay with Christ in his suffering, borne on my behalf and because of my sins.

+ *Method:* Contemplation, as on page 3.
I find myself in the courtyard of the house of Annas. I approach and feel the heat from the fire in the center of the courtyard. I am aware of the guards and servants who are present, and I watch their actions and listen to them. I pay particular attention to the feeling that charges the atmosphere.

To one side I see, and focus my attention on, Jesus, held prisoner by the guards. I become aware of his responses as the guards blindfold him and begin their taunting.

My attention shifts to Peter. I see his reaction to the situation and watch as the servants question him. I listen and watch sensitively as Peter denies Jesus and fellowship with the disciples.

I hear the cock crow. I see Jesus turn toward Peter. I allow myself time to fully absorb Jesus' look at Peter. I allow myself to receive the look of Jesus as he turns to me.

+ *Closing:* (Review the Colloquy section on page 10.)
I speak with Jesus, sharing with him my sorrow for my denials of him, my gratitude for his unconditional love.

I close with the Our Father.

+ *Review of Prayer:* I record in my journal whatever insights or feelings have surfaced during my period of prayer.

Week 3, Day 5: The Bound Prisoner

LUKE 22:66–23:1

When day broke there was a meeting of the elders of the people, attended by the chief priests and scribes. He was brought before their council, • and they said to him, "If you are the Christ, tell us." "If I tell you," he replied "you will not believe me, • and if I question you, you will not answer. • But from now on, the Son of Man will be seated at the right hand of the Power of God." • Then they all said, "So you are the Son of God then?" He answered, "It is you who say I am." "What need of witnesses have we now?" they said. "We have heard it for ourselves from his own lips." • The whole assembly then rose, and they brought him before Pilate.

The swaddled child of Bethlehem has become the bound prisoner before the Sanhedrin.

During the stillness of a tranquil Bethlehem night, in a cave which served as a manger, a woman gave birth to a son. From nearby fields, shepherds came. Filled with faith, they came to see the child whose birth had long been promised. Overjoyed at the sight of the child with his mother, the shepherds proclaimed that this child was, for all, the long-awaited realization of their hope, "Christ the Lord."

The swaddled child has become the bound prisoner.

In the predawn of a Jerusalem morning, the supreme council of official Judaism convenes. Projecting a facade of legal formality, the seventy members of the Sanhedrin are seated in a semicircle. Within the council, long-time enemies, the Sadducees and Pharisees, have found a common focus for their hostility.

"If you are the Christ, tell us."

Contempt and prejudice are palpable as they vindictively direct charges toward their victim.

At last, they have apprehended the one whom the people proclaim to be their promised messiah. The one whose presence they perceive as a threat to their power and influence stands before them.

How can this be?

The one proclaimed by God's angel to be the Son of God (Luke 1:36), the one whom God identified as his chosen one, his beloved Son (Luke 3:22), is now charged with claiming that sonship.

"So you are the Son of God then?"

How can this be?

Those who level the charge are the ones who publicly invest him with his identity!

"It is you who have said it."

Those who were to judge now become the judged.

In the presence of Jesus, offical Judaism is confronted with the reality that fulfills yet transcends it. Blinded in leadership, the members of the Sanhedrin are closed to the new paradigm Jesus offers. They ask the question but cannot hear the answer.

Jesus, however, is tranquil, confident of his innocence and trusting in God. He is, indeed, the Christ, Son of God and Son of Man!

"From now on," present to the Church, "seated at the right hand of . . . God," he is the source of transforming power.

Jesus' response to the Sanhedrin goes far beyond their questioning. His suffering transcends all history; his Spirit transforms all time.

The bound prisoner has become the source of liberation for all!

Suggested Approach to Prayer: Lord Jesus Christ

+ *Daily prayer pattern:* (See pages 1 and 2.)
   I quiet myself and relax in the presence of God.
   I declare my dependency on God.

+ *Grace:* I ask God to allow me to enter into sorrow as I stay with Christ in his suffering, borne on my behalf and because of my sins.

+ *Method:* Mantra, as on page 4.
   I relax and center deep within myself. I spiral downward to discover where it is that I most experience myself bound and unfree.

Aware of my own lack of freedom, I recite slowly and repeatedly, in the manner of a mantra, the prayer,

Lord Jesus Christ, Son of the living God,
have mercy on me, a sinner.

+ *Closing:* (Review the Colloquy section on page 10.)
I close my prayer by resting in Jesus' Spirit of merciful love.
I pray the Our Father.

+ *Review of Prayer:* I record in my journal whatever insight or feelings have surfaced during my period of prayer.

Week 3, Day 6: Repetition

Suggested Approach to Prayer:

+ *Daily prayer pattern:* (See pages 1 and 2.)
I quiet myself and relax in the presence of God.
I declare my dependency on God.

+ *Grace:* I ask God to allow me to enter into sorrow as I stay with Christ in his suffering, borne on my behalf and because of my sins.

+ *Method:* Repetition, as on page 6.
In preparation, I review my prayer periods since the last repetition day. I select for my repetition the period of prayer in which I was most deeply moved or the one in which I experienced a lack of emotional response, or one in which I was grasped with insight or experienced confusion. I use the method with which I approached the passage initially. I open myself to hear again God's word to me in that particular passage.

+ *Review of Prayer:* I write in my journal any feelings, experiences, or insights that have surfaced in this "second listening."

Week 4, Day 1: Suffered Under Pontius Pilate

MATTHEW 27:11–25

Jesus, then, was brought before the governor, and the governor put to him this question, "Are you the king of the Jews?" Jesus replied, "It is you who say it." • But when he was accused by the chief priests and the elders he refused to answer at all. • Pilate then said to him, "Do you not hear how many charges they have brought against you?" • But to the governor's complete amazement, he offered no reply to any of the charges.

At festival time it was the governor's practice to release a prisoner for the people, anyone they chose. • Now there was at that time a notorious prisoner whose name was Barabbas. • So when the crowds gathered, Pilate said to them, "Which do you want me to release to you: Barabbas, or Jesus who is called Christ?" • For Pilate knew it was out of jealousy that they had handed him over.

Now as he was seated in the chair of judgement, his wife sent him a message, "Have nothing to do with that man; I have been upset all day by a dream I had about him."

The chief priests and the elders, however, had persuaded the crowd to demand the release of Barabbas and the execution of Jesus. • So when the governor spoke and asked them, "Which of the two do you want me to release for you?" they said, "Barabbas." • "But in that case," Pilate said to them "what am I to do with Jesus who is called Christ?" They all said, "Let him be crucified!" • "Why?" he asked "What harm has he done?" But they shouted all the louder, "Let him be crucified!" • Then Pilate saw that he was making no impression, that in fact a riot was imminent. So he took some water, washed his hands in front of the crowd and said, "I am innocent of this man's blood. It is your concern."

"I found myself in a dim room" she began,

where a great number of people were assembled and appeared to be praying; but their words passed by me like murmuring water. Then, suddenly, it seemed as though my ears opened wide or as though the jet of a fountain were leaping from dark waters, and I heard distinctly the words, "suffered under Pontius Pilate, was crucified, died and was buried." I could not explain it to myself how my husband's name had come to be upon the lips of these people, nor what it might mean. Nevertheless, I felt an undefined dread upon hearing these words, as though they could have no other but some mysterious and ominous significance. (76, p. 10–11)

Gertrud von le Fort has imaginatively recreated the terror and panic that grips Claudia, the wife of Pilate, when she awakens from a dream in which she has seen future generations of people all praying the words of the creed.

Passing through the churches and cathedrals down the ages, Claudia hears, repeated over and over, her husband's guilt, "suffered under Pontius Pilate . . ." and is appalled.

The foreboding message of this dream moves her to send an urgent warning to Pilate, "Don't have anything to do with that innocent man."

His wife's warning comes to Pilate as he sits on the seat of judgment.

Pilate's interrogation of Jesus is complete, the ingeniousness of Jesus' non-commital responses has become obvious in the questioning. To Pilate's question, "Are you the king of the Jews?" Jesus' answer ambiguously affirms his messiahship.

Convinced of Jesus' innocence and believing that he is the victim of the Sanhedrin's envy, Pilate is inclined to set Jesus free, and Claudia's warning reiterates Pilate's own conviction.

In response to the formal charges of treason brought by the Jewish leaders, however, Jesus is silent.

Jesus' silence is significant in shaping the events that bring him to the cross. That silence stymies Pilate's efforts to release Jesus, and in the end, Pilate desperately turns to the crowd of pilgrims who fill the city for the celebration of Passover.

Despite the pervasive attitude of distrust and political unrest, Pilate appeals to the integrity of the people. Confident that they will choose Jesus, he invokes the custom of releasing a prisoner at Passover. He presents them with a choice between Jesus of Nazareth and a notorious terrorist, Barabbas. To his dismay, the crowd, swayed by the priests and elders, shout for the release of Barabbas.

Pilate is caught between his own conviction of Jesus' innocence and the crowd's irrational choice of Barabbas.

The crowd's hostility rises to new heights when Pilate questions them. Their fury mounts to the brink of riot as they explosively demand the most brutal form of Roman execution, crucifixion, for Jesus.

Yielding to the pressure of the mob, Pilate chooses an illusion of peace over simple justice. At the crossroads of critical decision, threatened by the radical message and way of Jesus, both Jew and Gentile capitulate to political expediency.

There is a nightmarish, Lady Macbeth quality in Pilate's attempt to purge himself of guilt by the ritual washing of his hands.

There is a grim and enduring tragedy in the people's arrogant assumption of Jesus' guilt.

There is a deep sadness in the death of Jesus, who was humiliated and rejected, "like a sheep that is dumb before its shearers / never opening its mouth" (Isa. 53:7).

He suffered under Pontius Pilate . . .

Suggested Approach to Prayer: The Creed

+ *Daily prayer pattern:* (See pages 1 and 2.)
   I quiet myself and relax in the presence of God.
   I declare my dependency on God.

+ *Grace:* I ask for the gift of being able to feel sorrow with Christ in sorrow, to be anguished with Christ's anguish, and even to experience tears and deep grief because of all the affliction Christ endures for me.

+ *Method:* Meditative Reading, as on page 5.
   I image myself in a great cathedral, one of the many people who have

made up the Christian community throughout the ages. I join my voice to those of the great choir as I pray slowly and meditatively the words of the Apostles' Creed.

Beginning with the words, "I believe in God . . ." I remain with each word of the prayer, gently repeating it for as long as it speaks to me, for as long as it touches me interiorly.

I continue this way through the text of the prayer. If any word or phrase seems particularly fruitful, I rest with its resonance, allowing myself to absorb the fullness of its direction and/or consolation.

> I believe in God, the Father Almighty, Creator of heaven and earth; and in Jesus Christ, His only Son, our Lord; who was conceived by the Holy Ghost, born of the Virgin Mary, suffered under Pontius Pilate, was crucified, died, and was buried. He descended into hell; the third day He arose again from the dead; He ascended into heaven, sits at the right hand of God, the Father Almighty; from thence He shall come to judge the living and the dead. I believe in the Holy Spirit, the holy catholic church, the communion of saints, the forgiveness of sins, the resurrection of the body, and life everlasting. Amen.

+ *Closing:* (Review the Colloquy section on page 10.)
I allow my heart to speak simply, openly to Jesus.
I pray the Our Father.

+ *Review of Prayer:* I record in my journal the feelings and insights that have surfaced during my period of prayer.

Week 4, Day 2: Silent Before Herod

LUKE 23:6–12

When Pilate heard this, he asked if the man were a Galilean; •
and finding that he came under Herod's jurisdiction he passed
him over to Herod who was also in Jerusalem at that time.
Herod was delighted to see Jesus; he had heard about
him and had been wanting for a long time to set eyes on him;
moreover, he was hoping to see some miracle worked by
him. • So he questioned him at some length; but without get-
ting any reply. • Meanwhile the chief priests and the scribes
were there, violently pressing their accusations. • Then
Herod, together with his guards, treated him with contempt
and made fun of him; he put a rich cloak on him and sent him
back to Pilate. • And though Herod and Pilate had been
enemies before, they were reconciled that same day.

"He made no reply." Jesus is silent; he is alone.

With each episode of his passion, as Jesus moves into his "hour," we see him become increasingly more isolated and silent.

He stands before Herod utterly without support. His disciples have deserted him, his own people have rejected him, and God is silent.

Again Jesus faces accusations and questions.

He is silent. He is innocent. There is no evidence to substantiate any wrongdoing. There is no defense for guiltlessness. To answer the questions of his accusers would be to betray who he is, who his God is, and the significance of this moment.

The moment calls for surrender and trust. Anything less than total acceptance would violate the integrity of his life and the absolute primacy of God. Silence is his only response.

Jesus is self-assured and composed in the situation. His silence is the strongest rebuke he can give to Herod.

Whatever Pilate's reasons for sending Jesus to Herod, whether from fear, or to flatter Herod, or simply to rid himself of Jesus, Herod is filled only with curiosity and contempt. Refusing to take Jesus seriously, Herod makes a joke of the incident.

Herod is unable to prove or disprove the accusations against Jesus, and after he and his soldiers have had "their fun," Herod sends Jesus back to Pilate robed in a ceremonial cloak. Ironically, the garment is less a statement of mockery and guilt than it is an eloquent sign of Jesus' innocence. Neither Herod nor Pilate can prove Jesus guilty, and neither can release him. In the mutuality of their powerlessness they forge a tenuous bond.

The passion of Jesus continues to unfold. Progressively, he is more alone, more silent. As he approaches his final surrender, the silence of Jesus encounters ever more deeply the silence of God (46, p. 181).

Suggested Approach to Prayer: Entry into Silence

+ *Daily prayer pattern:* (See pages 1 and 2.)
  I quiet myself and relax in the presence of God.
  I declare my dependency on God.

+ *Grace:* I ask for the gift of being able to feel sorrow with Christ in sorrow, to be anguished with Christ's anguish, and even to experience tears and deep grief because of all the afflictions Christ endures for me.

+ *Method:* Contemplation, as on page 3.
  I see Jesus as he is brought before Herod. I image, in detail, the palace room in which they meet. I am aware of how Jesus' dress and demeanor is in sharp contrast to Herod and his surroundings.

  I look at Herod and note his facial expression as he meets Christ and proceeds to question him. I take note of the tone of his questions, his anger, curiosity, malice.

  I see the chief priests and scribes who are present and listen to their violent accusations.

  I observe Jesus' face as he is subjected to the interrogation and accusations.

83

I see Jesus, silent.

I enter into the silence of Jesus as into a room of deep quiet and stillness. I allow myself to surrender to this silence.

So far as I am able, I allow the experience of the silence to be given expression through my five senses, asking myself

- what color or hue is the mood of Jesus' silence?
- what is the "sound" of this silence . . . the scent?
- what does this silence taste like, feel like?

I allow the silence of Jesus to fill my whole being.

+ *Closing:* (Review the Colloquy section on page 10.)
I speak with Jesus and stay with him through everything that happens.
I close the period of prayer with the Our Father.

+ *Review of Prayer:* I record in my journal the feelings and insights that have surfaced during my prayer.

Week 4, Day 3: Truth on Trial

JOHN 18:33–38; 19:1–12

So Pilate went back into the Praetorium and called Jesus to him, "Are you the king of the Jews?" he asked. • Jesus replied, "Do you ask this of your own accord, or have others spoken to you about me?" • Pilate answered, "Am I a Jew? It is your own people and the chief priests who have handed you over to me: what have you done?" • Jesus replied, "Mine is not a kingdom of this world; if my kingdom were of this world, my men would have fought to prevent my being surrendered to the Jews. But my kingdom is not of this kind." • "So you are a king then?" said Pilate. "It is you who say it" answered Jesus. "Yes, I am a king. I was born for this, I came into the world for this: to bear witness to the truth; and all who are on the side of truth listen to my voice." • "Truth?" said Pilate "What is that?"; and with that he went out again to the Jews and said, "I find no case against him."

Pilate then had Jesus taken away and scourged; • and after this, the soldiers twisted some thorns into a crown and put it on his head, and dressed him in a purple robe. • They kept coming up to him and saying, "Hail, king of the Jews!"; and they slapped him in the face.

Pilate came outside again and said to them, "Look, I am going to bring him out to you to let you see that I find no case." • Jesus then came out wearing the crown of thorns and the purple robe. Pilate said, "Here is the man." • When they saw him the chief priests and the guards shouted, "Crucify him! Crucify him!" Pilate said, "Take him yourselves and crucify him: I can find no case against him." • "We have a Law," the Jews replied "and according to that Law he ought to die, because he has claimed to be the Son of God."

*When Pilate heard them say this his fears increased. •
Re-entering the Praetorium, he said to Jesus, "Where do you
come from?" But Jesus made no answer. • Pilate then said to
him, "Are you refusing to speak to me? Surely you know I
have power to release you and I have power to crucify you?"
• "You would have no power over me" replied Jesus "if it had
not been given you from above; that is why the one who
handed me over to you has the greater guilt."*

*From that moment Pilate was anxious to set him free,
but the Jews shouted, "If you set him free you are no friend of
Caesar's; anyone who makes himself king is defying Caesar."*

A king is crowned! A king is robed in regal glory! Subjects render their
master homage and praise!

His crown is a bloody diadem of twisted thorns, sharply pressed into the flesh
of his scalp. His robe is a common red cloak of a soldier, worn and faded; the
"homage" he receives is accompanied, contemptuously, by slapping blows.

Ironically, this vulgar mimicry of a royal investiture speaks a profound truth.
A king *is* crowned!

The soldiers' grotesque parody serves, unconsciously, to unveil the truth that
some of the Jews reject and Pilate compromises. In spite of their crude and obtuse
ignorance, the soldiers do, in reality, declare the kingship of Christ.

Not only this mock coronation but the entire trial of Jesus is a travesty of
justice over which Pilate presides.

During the trial of Jesus, Pilate's incompetent leadership reaches its lowest
ebb. Marked by years of unsympathetic treatment of the Jewish people and their
beliefs, Pilate's position as governor is in constant jeopardy as the people of Judea
wait in alertness to report his next false step to Rome.

Having lost touch with his own inner truth, and face to face with the clarity
and strength of Jesus, Pilate is trapped by indecision. If the words of Jesus puzzle
Pilate, then Jesus' silence overwhelms him. Pilate vacillates!

Unable to condemn Jesus, unable to release him, Pilate regresses, yielding to
evil.

Pilate is caught in a trap of his own making, in a dilemma of powerlessness. Deeply rooted fear and insecurity prevent him from acting in truth. His spirit dulled and calloused by years of insensitivity, Pilate surrenders Jesus to death.

In handing Jesus over, Pilate rejects truth; he denies the truth of his own being. He betrays the law of truth that is basic to all human justice.

Pilate rejects the man who said, "I am . . . the Truth" (John 14:6).

The travesty of this trial ends as it began, with the cruel parody of royal acclamation, "Here is the man. . . . Here is your king" (John 19:6,15).

Once more, in ignorance, truth is spoken.

Standing vulnerably before the rabble, scourged and humiliated, the man Jesus *is* king. His truth and his witness to truth are our entrance into the kingdom.

The power of the kingdom is the spirit of the Risen Christ seen in the strength of truth as it continues to break through human limitation and sin.

From the cross of Christ, the words of Pilate, written two thousand years ago, proclaim today the truth at the heart of all human history, "Jesus the Nazarene, King of the Jews" (John 19:20).

Suggested Approach to Prayer: Jesus, Mocked and Rejected

+ *Daily prayer pattern:* (See pages 1 and 2.)
  I quiet myself and relax in the presence of God.
  I declare my dependency on God.

+ *Grace:* I ask for the gift to be able to feel sorrow with Christ in sorrow, to be anguished with Christ's anguish, and even to experience tears and deep grief because of all the afflictions Christ endures for me.

+ *Method:* Contemplation, as on page 3.
  Slowly and prayerfully I reread the passage.
  I choose one person in the passage whose role I will assume, perhaps a soldier, or someone in the crowd.
  I picture the city of Jerusalem, its streets filled with the milling crowds who have come to celebrate Passover.
  I see the crowd that has assembled near the Praetorium where Pilate is

conducting his interrogation of Jesus. I image the building, the details of its archi-
tecture, the flagstone terrace, the arched gates . . .

Intently, I look at Pilate. I take note of his clothing, which symbolizes his
office. I am aware of how his physical bearing reveals his inner attitude, and I
listen as he questions Jesus, aware of the tone of his interrogation.

"Are you the king of the Jews?"

I closely observe Jesus, as he makes his response. I am aware of how his
silences and responses deeply reveal the truth.

I continue my prayer following the dialogue.

As the people scream out for Barabbas, I note the expression on Jesus'
face.

I go with Jesus as he is taken away to be scourged and am present as the
soldiers crown him with thorns and mock him.

I continue to be aware of Jesus' pain and humiliation.

I follow Jesus as Pilate leads him out before the people and places him
on public display.

As the dialogue between Pilate and Jesus continues, I am sensitive to the
struggle within Pilate's spirit and the pathos of Jesus' rejection. I see Pilate hand
Jesus over to be crucified.

+ *Closing:* (Review the Colloquy section on page 10.)
I speak to Jesus and stay with him through everything that happens.
I pray the Our Father.

+ *Review of Prayer:* I write in my journal whatever feelings or insights have
surfaced during this period of prayer.

Week 4, Day 4: Good Friday Journey

JOHN 19:13–22

Hearing these words, Pilate had Jesus brought out, and seated himself on the chair of judgement at a place called the Pavement, in Hebrew Gabbatha. • It was Passover Preparation Day, about the sixth hour. "Here is your king" said Pilate to the Jews. • "Take him away, take him away!" they said. "Crucify him!" "Do you want me to crucify your king?" said Pilate. The chief priests answered, "We have no king except Caesar." • So in the end Pilate handed him over to them to be crucified.

They then took charge of Jesus, • and carrying his own cross he went out of the city to the place of the skull or, as it was called in Hebrew, Golgotha, • where they crucified him with two others, one on either side with Jesus in the middle. • Pilate wrote out a notice and had it fixed to the cross; it ran: "Jesus the Nazarene, King of the Jews." • This notice was read by many of the Jews, because the place where Jesus was crucified was not far from the city, and the writing was in Hebrew, Latin and Greek. • So the Jewish chief priests said to Pilate, "You should not write 'King of the Jews,' but 'This man said: I am King of the Jews.'" • Pilate answered, "What I have written, I have written."

Thousands of women, men, and children make their way along the narrow streets of old Jerusalem. Some are singing, some are praying aloud, and some walk in total silence.

The day is Good Friday.

Around the earth in churches everywhere on Good Friday, people make an imaginary journey down these same streets.

Whether in the streets of Jerusalem or in the aisles of a church, all these people carry within their hearts a vision of holiness, the *mysterium tremendum*, and *mysterium fascinans* (24, p. 9). It is a vision so gripping that one is simultaneously repelled by and drawn into it. In these gatherings each one knows that he or she has an intimate share in the drama that is unfolding.

That drama is *the Way of the Cross.*

"Good" Friday is the time when Christian people come before the crucified Jesus. They come with a deep desire to discover within his suffering a meaning for their own brokenness and that of the world around them.

As they, in spirit, accompany Jesus on the way to Calvary, they are aware of the weight of his cross. Just as Isaac, the beloved son, carried the wood for his own sacrifice (Gen. 22:1–8), so, too, Jesus carries the heavy cross of his own sacrifice.

As the people enter into the way of the cross, they encounter in prayer the long history of promise and prophecy that Jesus' life embodies.

The event is Passover, the annual celebration of the liberation of the Hebrew nation from the bondage of Egypt. Significantly, Jesus' life is handed over at the precise hour that the passover lambs were killed in the Temple. At that hour, the Jewish people recalled how, twelve hundred years before, at the first Passover, the blood of a sacrificed lamb marked the doors of their ancestors, who were spared from death.

Now, in the surrender of Jesus, we see the new Passover, the passage of Jesus through death into new life. He is "like a lamb that is led to the slaughter-house" (Isa. 53:7).

Teresa of Avila counsels us to "fix our eyes on the crucified" (77, p. 196).

Here the Christian discovers that the endurance and faithfulness of Jesus to his role and mission is the transforming power that enables his followers to carry their own particular cross.

The words of Saint Paul are further encouragement:

We are in difficulties on all sides, but never cornered; we see no answer to our problems, but never despair; • we have been persecuted, but never deserted; knocked down, but never killed; • always, wherever we may be, we carry with us in our body the death of Jesus, so that the life of Jesus, too, may always be seen in our body. • Indeed, while we are still alive, we are consigned to our death every day, for the sake of Jesus, so that in our mortal flesh the life of Jesus, too, may be openly shown. . . . knowing that he who raised the Lord Jesus to life will raise us with Jesus in our turn. . . . (2 Cor. 4:8–11,14).

Suggested Approach to Prayer: The Way of the Cross

+ *Daily prayer pattern:* (See pages 1 and 2.)
I quiet myself and relax in the presence of God.
I declare my dependency on God.

+ *Grace:* I ask for the gift to be able to feel sorrow with Christ in his sorrow, to be anguished with Christ's anguish, and even to experience tears and deep grief because of all the afflictions Christ endures for me.

+ *Method:* Meditation, as on page 2.
Using the exercise, The Way of the Cross (on the next two pages), I enter into the journey of Jesus from his presence before Pilate to Calvary and even to the empty tomb of Easter morning. I bring to the sufferings of Jesus my own sharing of pain as a participation ". . . in my own body to do what I can to make up all that is still to be undergone by Christ for the sake of his body, the Church" (Col. 1:24).

+ *Closing:* (Review the Colloquy section on page 10.) I simply stay with Jesus in silence, or speak to him from my heart.

+ *Review of Prayer:* In my journal, I record the "station" that has most touched me in this prayer.

1. As Jesus appears before Pilate, I remember a time when I experienced being misunderstood, condemned:

2. As Jesus receives his cross, I recall a time when I received a cross into my life:

5. As Simon helps Jesus carry his cross, I consider who has been there to lift the cross from my shoulders, from my heart:

3. As Jesus falls the first time, I remember when I first experienced failure, my own limits:

6. As Veronica wipes the face of Jesus, I remember the Veronicas in my life—those who stood by me, comforted me, even at the risk of their own rejection:

4. As Mary encourages Jesus, I remember someone who encouraged me to follow God's call; I remember how she or he looked at me:

7. As Jesus falls a second time, I recall the times when I have experienced the helplessness of falling, knowing that I would fall again, and again:

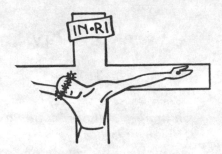

8. As the women reach out to comfort Jesus, I remember the faces of those whom I have reached out to comfort, even in my own pain:

9. As Jesus falls a third time, I recall a time when I felt as if I had fallen and could not go on:

10. As Jesus is stripped of his clothing, I remember the experience of feeling so poor, so stripped, so vulnerable before others:

11. As I see Jesus nailed to the cross, I consider what it is that fastens me to the cross of Jesus Christ:

12. As I image Jesus dying on the cross, I recall the circumstances, the interior call to love unconditionally, to be forgiving even when there seems to be no return:

13. As I image Mary holding the dead body of her Son, I hold in loving memory those who received me in my pain and grieved with me:

14. As Jesus' body is laid in the tomb, I consider what it is in my life that most holds me entombed, where I most experience death:

15. As I become aware of the empty tomb of Easter morning, I am aware not only of the pain of my life, but of the new life, emerging and deepening within me:

Week 4, Day 5: King and Priest

JOHN 19:23–24

When the soldiers had finished crucifying Jesus they took his clothing and divided it into four shares, one for each soldier. His undergarment was seamless, woven in one piece from neck to hem; • so they said to one another, "Instead of tearing it, let's throw dice to decide who is to have it." In this way the words of scripture were fulfilled:

> They shared out my clothing among them.
> They cast lots for my clothes.

This is exactly what the soldiers did.

"In his body lives the totem spirit of the tribe" (75, p. 37).

These words surely can be applied to Jesus. For Jesus, as king *and* priest, embodies the life of his people, God's own Spirit.

In his crucifixion, Jesus is flagrantly displayed! Above his head the title, "King of the Jews," simultaneously extols and condemns him, while at his feet, soldiers gamble to see who will win the priest-like garment, his seamless tunic.

Suspended in stark vulnerability between heaven and earth, Jesus—king and priest—unites the secular and the sacred, chaos and cosmos, creator and creature, feminine and masculine, body and spirit.

Wounded, Jesus is the healer of all that is disembodied. The sufferings of Jesus are the means by which all things are reconciled to each other and to God. Through the cross, the *conjunctio oppositorum*, the marriage of opposites, is effected.

In Jesus, all of humanity is thrust forward out of its slumbering darkness into the awakening of holy consciousness.

"Night truly blessed when heaven is wedded to earth and [all] is reconciled with God!" (54, Easter vigil, p. 184).

Suggested Approach to Prayer: Before the Cross

+ *Daily prayer pattern:* (See pages 1 and 2.)
I quiet myself and relax in the presence of God.
I declare my dependency on God.

+ *Grace:* I ask for the gift of being able to feel sorrow with Christ in sorrow, to be anguished with Christ's anguish, and even to experience tears and deep grief because of all the afflictions Christ endures for me.

+ *Method:* Contemplation, as on page 3 and Mantra, page 4.
I take my cross or crucifix in my hands and look at it closely. Before me I see Jesus hanging there. I contemplate each of his hands splayed open by the nails. I am aware of the bruises across his shoulders.
I look long at his head and face, framed by thorns.
I see his feet pierced and fastened to the cross.
Above his head is the title, "King of the Jews."
I am aware of the starkness of his nakedness.
I remain with Jesus in his vulnerability, taking note of the feelings that surface within me.

+ *Closing:* (Review the Colloquy section on page 10.)
I allow my heart to speak to Jesus, king and priest, in my own words, or through a mantra such as, "Lord Jesus Christ, king and priest, receive my spirit."
I pray the Our Father.

+ *Review of Prayer:* I note in my journal whatever feelings or insights have surfaced during this time of prayer.

Week 4, Day 6: Repetition

Suggested Approach to Prayer

+ *Daily prayer pattern:* (See pages 1 and 2.)
I quiet myself and relax in the presence of God.
I declare my dependency on God.

+ *Grace:* I ask God to allow me to enter into a sorrow as I stay with Christ in his suffering, borne on my behalf and because of my sins.

+ *Method:* Repetition, as on page 6.
In preparation, I review my prayer periods since the last repetition day. I select for my repetition the period of prayer in which I was most deeply moved or the one in which I experienced a lack of emotional response, or one in which I was grasped with insight or experienced confusion. I use the method with which I approached the passage initially. I open myself to hear again God's word to me in that particular passage.

+ *Review of Prayer:* I write in my journal any feelings, experiences, or insights that have surfaced in this "second listening."

my God,
my God,
why
have you
deserted me?
Matthew 27:46

Week 5, Day 1: Stretched Between Opposites

LUKE 23:39–43

One of the criminals hanging there abused him. "Are you not the Christ?" he said. "Save yourself and us as well." • But the other spoke up and rebuked him. "Have you no fear of God at all?" he said. "You got the same sentence as he did, but in our case we deserved it: we are paying for what we did. But this man has done nothing wrong. • Jesus," he said "remember me when you come into your kingdom." • "Indeed, I promise you," he replied "today you will be with me in paradise."

There is an ancient Jewish saying that "man enters this world with fist clenched, as if all the world were his to own; he leaves it with hands spread open, as if he wanted to say that he no longer possessed any of the things he once cherished" (57, p. 253).

The two thieves crucified on either side of Jesus have lived their lives with clenched fists. Even so, in this, their last moment, each has a choice—to mockingly seek a reprieve, or to dare to change.

At the gate of death the choice is made. In the presence of Jesus, one thief challenges, the other one believes.

Between the challenger and the believer, Jesus is stretched taut!

We look at the two thieves and we see ourselves. We see our positive side and our dark, negative side. We readily identify and claim our positive "thief." He is easy to own and to love. He is always open, sincere, trusting, and desirous to be and to do good.

The dark "thief" is not so easy to accept; in fact, he is often hidden, so well disguised that we are unable to recognize him for what he is. To acknowledge and accept these "thieves," these opposites within us, is to begin to envision a new and more complete sense of self.

To live dynamically poised between the conflicting poles within us, is, paradoxically, to experience freedom.

Through the cross of Jesus, the energy of the opposites becomes channeled and transformed into power for life.

In the reality of the historical Jesus nailed to a cross, we see no longer the division of opposites but the reconciling balance of chthonic and numinous creativity. Christ crucified represents oneness—the unity of the right and the left, the below and the above.

It is only *through* the crucified Jesus that reconciliation of opposites is possible. One thief says yes to Jesus; the other tragically rejects him. To look at Jesus crucified is to see the horror of this sin of rejection. Crucified between the two thieves, Jesus experiences this rejection—physically, psychically, and spiritually.

To fix our eyes on Jesus is to be irrevocably drawn into the passion. Through him we experience our own unique "stretching" between "the thieves," the opposites within us.

In this inner passion a new awareness of the reality of the evil within us surfaces. Focused on Jesus, however, we need not be afraid of this painful encounter. We can trust that the "rejecting thief" does not speak the last word for us.

Our "good thief" also insists on making his voice heard! His courageous yes to Jesus opens us to hear and to receive our own beauty and goodness as it seeks full expression.

This entry into our personal passion is, however, not without danger. The threat of becoming overwhelmed is very real. Upon meeting our evil side we may succumb to the temptation of despair, or, on discovering the depth of our goodness, we may yield to the seduction of self-satisfaction.

Our safety through this difficult passion-passage depends on our maintaining a concentrated stillness, which is centered in Jesus.

The ultimate word of the passion of Jesus is the word of love. The love of God for Jesus and the love of Jesus for God is the force that sustains Jesus as he hangs on the cross. This energy of love allows Jesus to reach out in his own pain to beg God's compassion not only for the confessing thief but for all those who have rejected and crucified him. "Father, forgive them; they do not know what they are doing" (Luke 23:34).

His love knows no limits. When the thief asks merely to be remembered, Jesus responds with unlimited love, "Today you will be with me in paradise."

Jesus promises the thief far more than he would ever have hoped.

For the thief and for us, the outstretched body of Jesus is the great host of new life; his cross is the centering mandala through which is released the transforming, reconciling power of love.

Suggested Approach to Prayer: Promise of Paradise

+ *Daily prayer pattern:* (See pages 1 and 2.)
I quiet myself and relax in the presence of God.
I declare my dependency on God.

+ *Grace:* I ask for the gift of being able to feel sorrow with Christ in sorrow, to be anguished with Christ's anguish, and even to experience tears and deep grief because of the afflictions Christ endures for me.

+ *Method:* Contemplation, as on page 3.
I image myself at the scene of the crucifixion. I attend to the atmosphere around me—the darkness of the day, the confusion of the mob, the general mood . . .

I note, on either side of Jesus, two others who are being crucified. I become conscious of their pain, their facial expressions, their words.

I see them observe Jesus and note their opposite responses and how their inner attitudes are portrayed through their words and the tone of their voices. I note the abuse and ridicule of the one and the basic honesty and belief of the other.

Prayerfully, I reflect on how these opposite responses to Jesus are present today . . . in the world, within me.

I see Jesus respond to the humble request of the one thief. Listening to Jesus' promise, I allow it to resonate deeply within me.

+ *Closing:* (Review the Colloquy section on page 10.)
I stay with Jesus and speak to him from my heart.
I pray the Our Father.

+ *Review of Prayer:* I note in my journal how I experience the tension of opposites within me.

Week 5, Day 2: From Mother to Woman

JOHN 19:25–27

Near the cross of Jesus stood his mother and his mother's sister, Mary the wife of Clopas, and Mary of Magdala. • Seeing his mother and the disciple he loved standing near her, Jesus said to his mother, "Woman, this is your son." • Then to the disciple he said, "This is your mother." And from that moment the disciple made a place for her in his home.

From "mother" to "woman." Mary heard her son, who had all his life called her "mother," now in his hour of death, address her as "woman."

The only other time Jesus called Mary "woman" was at the wedding feast in Cana, when she pleaded with him to respond to the bridal couple's embarrassment at having run out of wine. Then he replied to her, "Woman, why turn to me? My hour has not come yet" (John 2:4).

Jesus did, however, respond to his mother's request; he met the couple's need by turning water into wine. That transformation of water into wine was the first of Jesus' great miracles. It was a powerful sign and a promise of the joy and fulfillment that the new age of Jesus would herald.

Now, on Calvary, his hour *has* come; the promise is being fulfilled.

In calling his mother "woman," Jesus symbolically names and establishes, with great dignity, her role in the new age. Jesus confirms her identity when he confides John, the representative of all believers, to Mary. At this moment Mary's physical motherhood of Jesus, like the water changed to wine, is transformed.

From this time forward, she will be the mother of all believers, "mother of the church" (1, The Church, p. 86, note 262).

Mary is, like the first woman, mother of all the living (Gen. 3:20). In the new creation, she is recognized as the "new Eve" (Ibid, para. 53, p. 88).

Eve brought forth her sons in pain (Gen. 3:16). Mary, also, must suffer the agony of birthing. Her labor as mother of the Church begins with the death of her son. It calls for her total surrender.

Mary stands at the foot of her son's cross. She is unable to relieve his agony. She does not completely understand the reason for his dying. Yet she stands!

In faith she remains near her son. Her steadfastness in this hour vividly recalls the faithfulness of her fiat, when she surrendered her body to God's will and made possible Jesus' birth. "Behold the handmaid of the Lord; let it be to me according to your word" (Luke 1:28).

She is the great mother in labor bringing forth the life of Jesus in the world. She is the woman who stands, in love, at the foot of every cross.

Suggested Approach to Prayer: Mantra of Mary

+ *Daily prayer pattern:* (See pages 1 and 2.)
   I quiet myself and relax in the presence of God.
   I declare my dependency on God.

+ *Grace:* I ask to share in the sufferings of Jesus, in the spirit of Mary.

+ *Method:* Mantra, as on page 4.

I image myself with Mary at the foot of the cross. I image in great detail the surroundings; for example, the time of day, the warmth or chill in the air, the people—soldiers, faithful women, the Pharisees, the simple onlookers. I note the expressions on their faces, perhaps curiosity, disbelief, fear, compassion, sorrow.

I look closely at Mary. I take note of the emotions that etch her face and posture . . . I especially note how all her attention is focused on Jesus as he hangs on the cross.

I, too, look at Jesus. I look intently at the muscles of his body, stretched taut, at the nails that have cruelly pierced his flesh, at the harshness of the crown of thorns . . . I see particularly the agony in his face, the pain in his eyes.

I see Jesus look directly into my eyes. I hear him say to me, "_____, behold your mother." I hear him say to Mary, of me, "Woman, behold your son/ daughter."

Here is Mary, whose steadfast loyalty and faithfulness to Jesus serves to nurture my own faith commitment to Jesus.

I pray, in mantra fashion, the words of Jesus:

_____, behold your mother.

Woman, behold your son/daughter.

Here is Mary, whose surrendering yes to God nurtures the inbreaking of new creation and hope within me.

_____, behold your mother.

Woman, behold your son/daughter.

Here is Mary, whose love openly welcomes and nurtures me within the community of Christ's body, the Church.

_____, behold your mother.

Woman, behold your son/daughter.

Here is Mary, whose concern for my human needs nurtures an openness to God's transforming power within me.

_____, behold your mother.

Woman, behold your son/daughter.

Here is Mary, whose willingness to stand at the foot of the cross nurtures me to risk and to endure the suffering of my particular circumstances in life, my share in her son's passion.

_____, behold your mother.

Woman, behold your son/daughter.

I continue to repeat, slowly and prayerfully, the words of Jesus, as a mantra, as long as they continue to nourish me.

+ *Closing:* (Review the Colloquy section on page 10.)

I thank Jesus for the gift of his mother, the woman who stands at the foot of the cross.

I pray the Hail Mary.

+ *Review of Prayer:* I record in my journal the images of this time of prayer that have most deeply touched me.

Week 5, Day 3: One of Us

JOHN 19:28–29

After this, Jesus knew that everything had now been completed, and to fulfill the scripture perfectly he said:

"I am thirsty."

A jar full of vinegar stood there, so putting a sponge soaked in the vinegar on a hyssop stick they held it up to his mouth.

"I thirst."

Jesus' poignant cry from the cross speaks strongly to us of his humanness.

If there is any time when the humanness of Jesus is undeniably apparent, it is as he hangs on the cross. It is impossible to look at him crucified or to listen to his human cry of thirst and not realize that Jesus is radically one of us, that he, God's Son, has been "injected" into our humanness, into our world.

The amazing reality of Jesus, God's Son, actually being one of us is what enables him to effect for us the work that the Creator has entrusted to him.

This work is the work of unification.

"May they all be one.
Father, may they be one in us,
as you are in me and I am in you,
so that the world may believe it was you who sent me."
(John 17:21)

The inner thirst of Jesus, and our thirst, too, is the deep and intense longing within each of us for this oneness with each other and oneness in God.

This yearning for union is the evolutionary pull that inevitably draws all of creation upward and forward toward the new creation, the lived reality of God's presence in our world.

The cross is the symbol of hope and emergence. The suffering and death of Jesus not only heals our brokenness but transforms it, opening us in receptivity to the power of the Risen Christ. Suffering overcomes all resistance to the entry of

Christ's spirit within us. The cross is a profound symbol of the love-work of the Creator lived out in the struggle and pain of daily life.

This labor of love offers no escape from suffering. The Christian, like Christ, must endure the thirst for communion which is, paradoxically, the energy of the cross.

Jesus says, "I thirst."

We say, "I thirst."

"The Spirit and the Bride say, 'Come.' Let everyone who listens answer, 'Come.' *Then let all who are thirsty come:* all who want it may *have the water* of life, *and have it free*" (Rev. 22:17).

Suggested Approach to Prayer: I Thirst

+ *Daily prayer pattern:* (See pages 1 and 2.)
I quiet myself and relax in the presence of God.
I declare my dependency on God.

+ *Grace:* I ask for the gift of being able to feel the inner thirst that was a poignant part of Jesus' passion.

+ *Method:* Meditation, as on page 2.
Prayerfully, I reread John 19:28–29. I image the thirst of Christ and hear his cry.

In answering the following questions, I bring my thirst to Christ.

• As a child, what did I thirst for?

• What have the experiences of my life revealed to me about my thirst?

• What do I want my experience of thirst to be?

• What does all this say to me about myself, my thirst, my journey?

As I contemplate the thirst of Jesus, I consider how his thirst, in suffering, speaks to me and my life circumstances.

+ *Closing:* (Review the Colloquy section on page 10.)
I speak to Christ and stay with him through everything that happens.
I pray the Our Father.

+ *Review of Prayer:* I note in my journal whatever feelings or insights surface during my prayer.

Week 5, Day 4: The Cross—Catalyst

MATTHEW 27:39–44

The passers-by jeered at him; they shook their heads • and said, "So you would destroy the Temple and rebuild it in three days! Then save yourself! If you are God's son, come down from the cross!" • The chief priests with the scribes and elders mocked him in the same way. • "He saved others;" they said "he cannot save himself. He is the king of Israel; let him come down from the cross now, and we will believe in him. • He puts his trust in God; now let God rescue him if he wants him. For he did say, 'I am the son of God.'" • Even the robbers who were crucified with him taunted him in the same way.

Suffering is the meeting point between good and evil (37, p. 325).

As Jesus hangs on the cross, Satan once again makes his evil presence known. The mocking and the jeering is his voice; his mouthpiece is the crowd.

During the temptations in the desert (Matt. 4:1–11), the forces of evil and good, darkness and light, encountered each other. In this last moment of Jesus' suffering and death, they again come face to face.

Jesus is not spared this last temptation: "If you are God's son, come down." The Jewish leaders who choose to oppose Jesus see his helplessness on the cross as total powerlessness. Arrogantly, they interpret this as proof that Jesus cannot be the Messiah, God's Son. They hinge their belief on his meeting their demands for a miracle: "Come down and we will believe."

Christ does not come down from the cross. He does not yield to an ego-inflating display of power. Rather, enduring the pain, he remains firm in his trust and obedience to God.

In the power of this radical trust and obedience the true sonship of Jesus is shown. Only in the strength of such unlimited trust is Christ able to endure the intense suffering and degradation of his crucifixion.

By embracing the humiliation of human limitation, Jesus, God's Son, broke through, for us, the resistance that blocks the power of surrender and transformation.

"It would have been human to have come down from the cross; it was divine to hang there" (52, p. 348).

The historical cross of Jesus, the visible sign of his trust and obedience, catalyzes the release of God's power and goodness into our world.

Jesus is the working model for us as we search for meaning within the sufferings of our own lives. Jesus' surrender to the pain of the cross reassures us that our sufferings, like his, are part of the evolutionary process of all humankind. Suffering leads us, as it led Jesus, into the Easter oneness of love with each other and with God. Evil will not have the final word.

"The Christian is not asked to swoon in the shadow, but to climb in the light of the Cross" (71, p. 70).

Suggested Approach to Prayer: The Heart of Christ

+ *Daily prayer pattern:* (See pages 1 and 2.)
I quiet myself and relax in the presence of God.
I declare my dependency on God.

+ *Grace:* I ask for the gift to enter into the spirit of Jesus' passion, to share in the sorrow and anguish he endures for me.

+ *Method:* Contemplation, as on page 3.
I contemplate Jesus on the cross, noting his many sufferings. I hear the ridicule and the accusations hurled at him.

I focus my attention on Jesus' heart, his physical and spiritual center. In stillness, I concentrate all the energy of who I am on his heart.

Slowly I enter into the heart of Jesus as into a room. I am aware of any images or feelings that surface within me as I enter the heart of Christ.

I ask Jesus to show me his love that prompted him to endure the sufferings and humiliations of his cross.

I open myself to receive Jesus' sharing with me of his heart of love.

I focus my attention on Jesus' heart, which is filled with love. Gathered within his heart I see

- all my own sufferings and joys and desires to love and to be loved
- all those I love—husband, wife, sisters and brothers, children, friends, parents
- all those others for whom I am concerned—leaders of nations, the poor, prisoners, the homeless . . .

I image the heart of Jesus as the converging point of love in which all creation is drawn into unity.

I image the energy of this love flowing from and expanding to fill the entire world.

I see the vast expanse of love-energy moving all of creation forward into a future when Christ will be all in all.

+ *Closing:* (Review the Colloquy section on page 10.)

In my own words I express my gratitude to Jesus for having shared with me his vision and his love.

I pray the Our Father.

+ *Review of Prayer:* I write in my journal the insights and feelings that surfaced during my prayer.

Week 5, Day 5: Repetition

Suggested Approach to Prayer

+ *Daily prayer pattern:* (See pages 1 and 2.)
  I quiet myself and relax in the presence of God.
  I declare my dependency on God.

+ *Grace:* I ask God to allow me to enter into a sorrow as I stay with Christ in his sufferings, borne on my behalf and because of my sins.

+ *Method:* Repetition, as on page 6.

In preparation, I review my prayer periods since the last repetition day. I select for my repetition the period of prayer in which I was most deeply moved or the one in which I experienced a lack of emotional response, or one in which I was grasped with insight or experienced confusion. I use the method with which I approached the passage initially. I open myself to hear again God's word to me in that particular passage.

+ *Review of Prayer:* I write in my journal any feelings, experiences, or insights that have surfaced in this "second listening."

Week 5, Day 6: Cry of Distress

MATTHEW 27:45–50

From the sixth hour there was darkness over all the land until the ninth hour. • And about the ninth hour, Jesus cried out in a loud voice, "Eli, Eli, lama sabachthani?" that is, "My God, my God, why have you deserted me?" • When some of those who stood there heard this, they said, "The man is calling on Elijah," and one of them quickly ran to get a sponge which he dipped in vinegar and, putting it on a reed, gave it him to drink. • "Wait!" said the rest of them "and see if Elijah will come to save him." • But Jesus, again crying out in a loud voice, yielded up his spirit.

Jesus hangs on the cross. To the world he seems a failure, cursed by the law and devoid of all visible support (Gal. 3:13).

Jesus, who reassured his followers of God's faithful and intimate presence in their lives, is now abandoned.

Jesus, who performed so many miracles in God's name, is now without a sign.

Jesus, who brought to others the confidence that God responds to every prayer, now hears no word.

"My God, my God, why have you deserted me?"

This anguished cry of Jesus is one of distress, not despair (10, p. 194). He is being prematurely cut off from life; his mission, seemingly, aborted. He is scorned and rejected. Insidiously, the question must have arisen, "Have I lived in vain? Am I a failure?" Darkness covers the earth and enters his soul; the weight of the world's sin is heavy upon him.

Jesus' dying on the cross is a direct consequence of his life of total obedience. At every moment he has embraced what he discerned to be God's will for him.

Now in the agony of his last moments, an appeal to God is literally wrenched from the depths of his being.

111

Although we cannot know exactly what Jesus felt at that moment, clearly he was not spared the totally human and intense experience of isolation that accompanies imminent death. His distress was unquestionably real!

Yet one does not cry out if one does not expect to be heard. The moment of greatest desperation gives energy to the deepest truth, ". . . the heart being hard at bay, / is out with it!" (13, "Wreck of the Deutschland," 57–58).

"Eli, Eli, lama sabachthani?"

For those who do not believe, the cry of Jesus is misinterpreted and maliciously ridiculed.

Those who believe know it is God to whom Jesus calls out.

"My God, my God, why have you deserted me?"

These words recall the ancient Hebrew prayer wherein the distress and trust of the innocent sufferer are simultaneously held. The prayer of the psalmist is the spirit of the Christ.

> I call all day, my God, but you never answer,
> all night long I call and cannot rest.
> Yet, Holy One. . .
> in you our [ancestors] put their trust,
> they trusted and you rescued them;
> they called to you for help and they were saved,
> they never trusted you in vain.
>
> (Ps. 22:2–5)

Suggested Approach to Prayer: Psalm 22

+ *Daily prayer pattern:* (See pages 1 and 2.)
  I quiet myself and relax in the presence of God.
  I declare my dependency on God.

+ *Grace:* I ask for the gift to be able to feel sorrow with Christ in sorrow, to be anguished with Christ's anguish, and even to experience tears and deep grief because of all Christ endures for me.

+ *Method:* Meditative Reading, as on page 5.

112

I image myself with Jesus on Calvary. I am aware of his utter aloneness, of the absence of his disciples.

I see the scorn and hear the ridicule to which he is being subjected.

I am aware of the prevailing darkness of the day.

Looking at the face of Jesus, I become aware of the feelings portrayed in his expression. I hear Jesus' cry, and I allow it to echo within me. I am aware of the feelings that surface within me.

I pray Psalm 22 in the spirit of Jesus. I remain with each word of the psalm, gently repeating it for as long as it speaks to me, for as long as it touches me interiorly.

I proceed this way throughout the text of the psalm. If any word or phrase seems particularly fruitful, I rest with its resonance, allowing myself to absorb the fullness of its direction and/or consolation.

> My God, my God, why have you deserted me?
> Far from my prayer, from the words I cry?
> I call all day, my God, but you never answer;
> all night long I call and cannot rest.
> Yet, Holy One,
> you who make your home in the praises of Israel—
> in you our ancestors put their trust;
> they trusted and you rescued them.
> They called to you for help and were saved;
> they never trusted you in vain.
>
> Yet here I am, now more worm than human,
> scorn of all, jest of the people.
> All who see me jeer at me;
> they toss their heads and sneer:
> "You relied on Yahweh, let Yahweh save you!
> If Yahweh is your friend, let Yahweh rescue you!"
>
> Yet you drew me out of the womb;
> you entrusted me to my mother's breasts.
> You placed me on your lap from my birth,
> from my mother's womb you have been my God.

Do not stand aside: trouble is near
and I have no one to help me!

A herd of bulls surrounds me,
strong bulls of Bashan close in on me.
Their mouths are wide open for me,
like lions tearing and roaring.

I am like water draining away,
my bones are all disjointed,
and my heart is like wax
melting inside me.
My throat is drier than baked clay
and my tongue sticks to my mouth.

A pack of dogs surrounds me;
a gang of villains closes in on me.
They tie me hand and foot
and leave me lying in the dust of death.

I can count every one of my bones;
they glare and gloat over me.
They divide my garments among them
and cast lots for my clothes.

Do not stand aside, Yahweh.
O my strength, come quickly to my help;
rescue my soul from the sword,
my life from the grip of the dog.
Save me from the lion's mouth,
my poor soul from the wild bulls' horns!

Then I shall proclaim your name,
praise you in full assembly:
"You who fear Yahweh, praise God!
Entire race of Abraham and Sarah, glorify God!
Entire race of Israel, revere God!

For Yahweh has not despised
or disdained the poor in their poverty,
has not hidden from them,
but has answered when they called."

You are the theme of my praise in the Great Assembly;
I perform my vows in the presence of those who fear you.
The poor will eat and be satisfied.
Those who seek you will give praise.
Long life to their hearts!

The whole earth, from end to end,
will remember and come back to you;
all the families of the nations will bow down.
For you reign, the ruler of nations!
Before you all the prosperous of the earth will bow down;
before you will bow all who go down to the dust.
And my soul will live for you;
my children will serve you.
We will proclaim you to generations still to come,
your righteousness to a people yet unborn.
All this Yahweh has done.

+ *Closing:* (Review the Colloquy section on page 10.)
   I let my heart speak simply and openly to Jesus.
   I pray the Our Father.

+ *Review of Prayer:* I record in my journal the words and images of Psalm
22 that have most deeply touched me.

Week 6, Day 1: Into Your Hands

LUKE 23:44–46

It was now about the sixth hour and, with the sun eclipsed, a darkness came over the whole land until the ninth hour. • The veil of the Temple was torn right down the middle; • and when Jesus had cried out in a loud voice, he said, "Father, into your hands I commit my spirit." With these words he breathed his last.

It is a terrible thing to fall into the hands of the living God (64, p. 239). It is an awful—awe-filled—experience to find oneself within the embrace of a love that asks of us all we are, yet gives to us a fullness of love that is humanly incomprehensible.

Before the sheer mystery of such love, one is filled with reverence and fear.

On the cross, Jesus says yes to this love. The obedience to God which shaped Jesus' entire life climaxes in this final yes.

In spite of the intense physical suffering and aloneness, in spite of the human unknownness of what death itself holds, Jesus says yes.

As the incomprehensibility of God looms frighteningly before him, the yes of Jesus is an unconditional, total surrender.

He surrenders his entire being, his whole person. He surrenders himself to one who, in spite of the incomprehensibility, Jesus can still address as "Father."

Jesus lets go in love to the one who holds in love.

This love that releases Jesus into the presence of his Father releases power into our world. His yes is the evolutionary turning point of all creation. Through his surrender, the temple veil that separates the presence of God from human experience is torn open.

Through Jesus the heart of God is made visible. We, as followers of Jesus, are given access to enter as he did into God's love and to find ourselves, like him, in the hands of love.

Such love is, indeed, breathtaking!

Suggested Approach to Prayer: Mantra of Surrender

+ *Daily prayer pattern:* (See pages 1 and 2.)
I quiet myself and relax in the presence of God.
I declare my dependency on God.

+ *Grace:* I ask to enter deeply into the surrender of Jesus.

+ *Method:* Mantra, page 4.

. I take into my hands a cross or crucifix and fix my eyes upon it. I consider Jesus in his pain, as he is dying.

I ask to be open to hear the prayer of Jesus as he prayed it. I ask to share his experience of this moment in his life, so that the surrender that shaped his prayer may resonate deeply within me.

Gently and prayerfully, I allow the words of his prayer to become my own, as breathing in and out, I pray

Father, into your hands
I commit my spirit.

I image myself passing through the torn curtain of the Temple, entering into the holiness of Jesus. In his presence I continue to pray his prayer of surrender.

Father, into your hands
I commit my spirit.

+ *Closing:* (Review the Colloquy section on page 10.)
I speak to Christ simply, openly, offering to God my entire being.
I pray the Our Father.

+ *Review of Prayer:* I record in my journal the words of my offering, my surrender.

Week 6, Day 2: Jesus Is Lord

PHILIPPIANS 2:5–11

In your minds you must be the same as Christ Jesus:
> *His state was divine,*
> *yet he did not cling*
> *to his equality with God*
> *but emptied himself*
> *to assume the condition of a slave,*
> *and became as men are;*
> *and being as all men are,*
> *he was humbler yet,*
> *even to accepting death,*
> *death on a cross.*
> *But God raised him high*
> *and gave him the name*
> *which is above all other names*
> *so that* all beings
> *in the heavens, on earth and in the underworld,*
> should bend the knee *at the name of Jesus*
> *and that every tongue should acclaim*
> *Jesus Christ as lord,*
> *to the glory of God the Father.*

When spirit enters matter, matter becomes spirit.

Jesus' surrender on the cross is the ultimate moment of his entry into our humanity. His dying is the definitive revelation of his incarnation. Who would dare imagine that in God's plan the wisdom that stretched "from one end of the earth to the other" (Wisdom 8:1) would be unveiled in this man on a cross. Who would dare imagine the ramifications of such a God-event?

Before the crucified, our conception of God is turned upside down!

The God of thunder and fire (Exod. 19:16) hangs bound by nails.

The God whose word unleashed the energies of creation (Gen. 1) is silent before his accusers.

The God who is master of the universe is seen as servant of all (Isa. 52;53).

This image of a God, humiliated, weak, and vulnerable, is difficult to accept and certainly unpopular. A God of power, intellect, and wealth is far more palatable.

"And so, while the Jews demand miracles and the Greeks look for wisdom, here are we preaching a crucified Christ; to the Jews an obstacle that they cannot get over, to the pagans madness, . . ." (1 Cor. 1:22–23).

Our God, however, will not be limited by our self-serving notions of divinity. God presents to us, in the humanity of Jesus, a totality of presence that touches the deepest recesses of incomprehensible love.

In Jesus we are presented with the loving vulnerability of God, a vulnerability that paradoxically contains within it all power.

In Jesus we encounter God's own love-knowledge, which encompasses a wisdom that defies human articulation.

In Jesus we are offered a servanthood that promises the entire community of believers an authentic royalty.

". . . to those who have been called . . ." we preach "a Christ who is the power and the wisdom of God. For God's foolishness is wiser than human wisdom, and God's weakness is stronger than human strength" (1 Cor. 1:24–25).

A new door has been opened! It provides an entry into a new mode of being. It is good news for those who choose to place their trust in the God of love, especially for those who poignantly experience their own woundedness and poverty. And for those who have been snagged by pride, it is another chance.

The doorway to new life is the attitude of self-emptying that shaped the obedience of Jesus' life and death.

Jesus does not call us to a self-emptying that is a repression or negation of the self. He calls us to a voluntary surrender of power, a willingness to sink into the darkness of our own powerlessness and to encounter, within the negativity and void, the no-thingness that alone can reveal God.

Within this encounter with darkness, an option surfaces. One is unmercifully compelled to choose, to make the leap of surrender in trust and thereby opt for goodness, or failing, to remain fixated in indecision, an easy prey of evil.

Through the disobedience of the first Adam, we became divided and limited. Now, through the self-emptying obedience of the new Adam, Jesus, the door to freedom and reconciliation has been opened for us.

Because Jesus crucified *is* Lord, not only has the way been opened, but we have been given access to the gift of God's love, the healing power that transforms our darkness. The human condition that God embraced in Jesus and that is our inheritance is most profoundly experienced in this surrendering leap of trust.

In self-emptying surrender, darkness gives way to light and weakness is transformed into strength.

Before such love we, as human creatures, can only kneel and proclaim—with newfound joy—"Jesus is Lord."

Suggested Approach to Prayer: Jesus' Last Breath

+ *Daily prayer pattern:* (See pages 1 and 2.)
I quiet myself and relax in the presence of God.
I declare my dependency on God.

+ *Grace:* I ask to enter deeply into the spirit of Jesus' self-emptying surrender of love.

+ *Method:* Contemplation, as on page 3.
I image myself at the foot of the cross of Jesus. I see his suffering culminating in short gasps of breath. I see his chest expand as his lungs desperately strain for air. I see the pulse in his neck gradually weaken.

I remain with Jesus in these last moments.

I am aware of my feelings . . . of fear, desire to leave, sadness, regret, compassion, relief.

I am aware of any memories of Jesus' life and my relationship with him. I call to mind experiences I have had when I knew the reality of his presence and his love within me.

I become aware of any desires that surface within me—for example, to carry forward his mission . . . to reconcile with those I have wounded . . . to be faithful in the carrying of my own cross . . .

122

I continue to remain present in Jesus' final moments. I hear his final breath as he surrenders his spirit to God.

+ *Closing:* (Review the Colloquy section on page 10.)
I spend some moments in silence.
I pray the Our Father.

+ *Review of Prayer:* I record in my journal any insights or feelings that surface during this period of prayer.

Week 6, Day 3: Life and Spirit

JOHN 19:31–37

It was Preparation Day, and to prevent the bodies remaining on the cross during the sabbath—since that sabbath was a day of special solemnity—the Jews asked Pilate to have the legs broken and the bodies taken away. • Consequently the soldiers came and broke the legs of the first man who had been crucified with him and then of the other. • When they came to Jesus, they found he was already dead, and so instead of breaking his legs • one of the soldiers pierced his side with a lance; and immediately there came out blood and water. • This is the evidence of one who saw it—trustworthy evidence, and he knows he speaks the truth—and he gives it so that you may believe as well. • Because all this happened to fulfill the words of scripture:

Not one bone of his will be broken,

• *and again, in another place, scripture says:*

They will look on the one whom they have pierced.

The lance that pierces the dead Jesus releases life and spirit.

At the moment the soldier's lance penetrates Jesus' side, the heritage of the past and the legacy of Christ's Risen Spirit converge and are materialized in the sign of blood and water.

A rich mosaic of words and images that sustained and gave direction to God's chosen people provides an understanding of the profound symbolism in this scene.

The strongest Jewish Scriptures image within this episode is the paschal lamb, whose blood marked the doorposts and saved the Hebrew people from the angel of death (Exod. 12:7ff.). As the true paschal sacrifice, Jesus, servant of Yahweh, gives up his life; his blood is the saving power for his people (Isa. 53:6–7).

The ritual lamb had to be perfect, unblemished and without any broken bones (Exod. 12:46); likewise, Jesus' body is spared the mutilation of the customary breaking of bones that followed crucifixion.

The heart of the paschal lamb was slit open; the side of Jesus is pierced.

Jesus dies, signficantly, at the moment the lambs of sacrifice are being slaughtered in the Temple.

The import of this moment is amplified with the awareness that the temple of sacrifice is built upon the rock of Moriah, the site tradition identifies as the mountain to which Abraham brought his son Isaac to be sacrificed (Gen. 22:1–19).

This rock of Moriah, rock of sacrifice, has given way to the life-giving sacrifice of Jesus on Mount Calvary.

The life-imparting effect of his blood (Deut. 12:23) poured out for others is beautifully symbolized in the life-giving water, sign of the Spirit. As Moses, in the dryness of the desert passover (Exod. 17:1–7), drew water from the rock, the people of the Christian Scriptures draw water from Jesus, the "Rock" (1 Cor. 10:4).

And Jesus says, "If any [one] is thirsty, let him come to me!" (John 7:37).

Suggested Approach to Prayer: Lamb of God

+ *Daily prayer pattern:* (See pages 1 and 2.)
  I quiet myself and relax in the presence of God.
  I declare my dependency on God.

+ *Grace:* I ask to share deeply in the life and spirit of Jesus crucified.

+ *Method:* Contemplation, as on page 3, and Mantra, page 4.

I image myself at the foot of the cross. I see the dead body of Jesus hanging limply on the cross. I become as totally present as I can before Jesus.

I hear the soldiers approach and see them break the bones of those others who have been crucified with Jesus. I see a soldier approach Jesus and note his awareness that Jesus is already dead.

I see him plunge his lance into Jesus' side.

I see the blood and water flow from the wound.

I remain before Jesus, quiet within. Intermittently I pray interiorly the following:

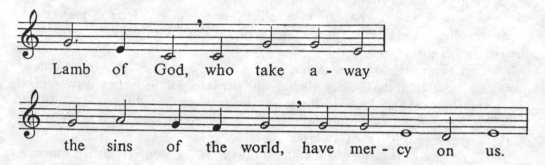

Lamb of God, who take a - way the sins of the world, have mer - cy on us.

+ *Closing:* (Review the Colloquy section on page 10.)
   I speak openly and simply to Christ whatever arises within me.
   I pray the Our Father.

+ *Review of Prayer:* I record in my journal whatever insights and feelings have surfaced during this time of prayer.

Week 6, Day 4: A Royal Burial

JOHN 19:38–42

After this, Joseph of Arimathaea, who was a disciple of Jesus —though a secret one because he was afraid of the Jews— asked Pilate to let him remove the body of Jesus. Pilate gave permission, so they came and took it away. • Nicodemus came as well—the same one who had first come to Jesus at night-time—and he brought a mixture of myrrh and aloes, weighing about a hundred pounds. • They took the body of Jesus and wrapped it with the spices in linen cloths, following the Jewish burial custom. • At the place where he had been crucified there was a garden, and in this garden a new tomb in which no one had yet been buried. • Since it was the Jewish Day of Preparation and the tomb was near at hand, they laid Jesus there.

Jesus was crowned a king; he was hailed and enthroned and proclaimed a king! True, his crown was one of thorns, his throne a cross, and mockery his royal acclamation.

Nonetheless, he is a king!

In his burial, the kingship previously denied Jesus in life is outwardly acknowledged. Inevitably the inner reality of Christ's kingship finally received a more fitting external expression. What was hidden comes to light.

Jesus' burial is lavish! He is given "a tomb with the rich" (Isa. 53:9), a new tomb surrounded by a private garden enclosure. The amount of spices with which his body is prepared is extraordinary, and the burial recalls the royal entombment of ancient kings (Neh. 3:16).

Interestingly, the generosity of two believers—Joseph of Arimathaea and Nicodemus who, up to the time of Jesus' death, had remained hidden, secret believers—makes visible the truth of Jesus' kingship. Joseph and Nicodemus show that even in the Sanhedrin and among the hostile Jewish opposition some believed in Jesus, yet remained silent because they feared ridicule and rejection.

Now, Joseph and Nicodemus come forward.

Even in the ultimate weakness of death, Jesus empowers the weak. Who but the weak and hidden can recognize a king who is weak and whose kingship is invisible.

It is the weak and the fearful among us (and within us) who, like Joseph and Nicodemus, see and claim in Christ the life and power of his kingship.

In the recognition and claiming of the power of Christ, weakness becomes strength.

"Now the life you have is hidden with Christ in God. But when Christ is revealed—and he is your life—you, too, will be revealed in all your glory with him" (Col. 3:3b–4).

Suggested Approach to Prayer: A New Tomb

+ *Daily prayer pattern:* (See pages 1 and 2.)
  I quiet myself and relax in the presence of God.
  I declare my dependency on God.

+ *Grace:* I ask for the gift of a passionate love for Christ, a love that will sustain me in life and death.

+ *Method:* Contemplation, as on page 3.
  I image myself in the garden that surrounds the tomb of Jesus. I see in detail the garden, the trees, the other foliage.

  I enter the tomb and am present before Jesus, who is prepared for burial. I see the white linen bands in which his body is wrapped. I am aware of the aroma of the spices and the fragrance of the oils that were used to anoint the body of Jesus.

  I contemplate the still, lifeless body of Jesus. I am aware of the tomb's deep silence.

  I consider meditatively the beauty of the garden enclosure, the freshness of this newly hewn tomb, and the extraordinary fragrance that surrounds me.

  I consider this man who was crucified in weakness and now buried in such splendor.

  I remain quietly in prayer.

+ *Closing:* (Review the Colloquy section on page 10.)

I allow my heart to speak to Jesus, thanking him for his great love and asking him to further reveal to me the meaning of this event. I close my prayer by rereading Colossians 3:3*b*–4.

I pray the Our Father.

+ *Review of Prayer:* I note in my journal whatever feelings and insights have surfaced during my prayer period.

Week 6, Day 5: Repetition

Suggested Approach to Prayer

+ *Daily prayer pattern:* (See pages 1 and 2.)
I quiet myself and relax in the presence of God.
I declare my dependency on God.

+ *Grace:* I ask for the gift of a deepening share of the self-emptying, surrendering love that sustained and moved Jesus to live and to die for us.

+ *Method:* Repetition, as on page 6.
Because of the importance of reflection on these past weeks of praying over the passion, the pray-er may desire to spend several days rereading his or her prayer journal in the manner of meditative reading.
It is further suggested that one or more periods of prayer be spent, allowing the effect of Christ's death to permeate one's being and to further see its energy, like light, spreading out and filling the world.

+ *Review of Prayer:* I write in my journal any feelings, experiences, or insights that have surfaced.

Week 6, Day 6: Labors of Love

ISAIAH 52:13–53:12

> *See, my servant will prosper,*
> *he shall be lifted up, exalted, rise to great heights.*
>
> *As the crowds were appalled on seeing him*
> *—so disfigured did he look*
> *that he seemed no longer human—*
> *so will the crowds be astonished at him,*
> *and kings stand speechless before him;*
> *for they shall see something never told*
> *and witness something never heard before:*
> *"Who could believe what we have heard,*
> *and to whom has the power of Yahweh been*
>   *revealed?"*
> *Like a sapling he grew up in front of us,*
> *like a root in arid ground.*
> *Without beauty, without majesty (we saw him),*
> *no looks to attract our eyes;*
> *a thing despised and rejected by men,*
> *a man of sorrows and familiar with suffering,*
> *a man to make people screen their faces;*
> *he was despised and we took no account of him.*
>
> *And yet ours were the sufferings he bore,*
> *ours the sorrows he carried.*
> *But we, we thought of him as someone punished,*
> *struck by God, and brought low.*
> *Yet he was pierced through for our faults,*
> *crushed for our sins.*
> *On him lies a punishment that brings us peace,*
> *and through his wounds we are healed.*

We had all gone astray like sheep,
each taking his own way,
and Yahweh burdened him
with the sins of all of us.
Harshly dealt with, he bore it humbly,
he never opened his mouth,
like a lamb that is led to the slaughter-house,
like a sheep that is dumb before its shearers
never opening its mouth.

By force and by law he was taken;
would anyone plead his cause?
Yes, he was torn away from the land of the living;
for our faults struck down in death.
They gave him a grave with the wicked,
a tomb with the rich,
though he had done no wrong
and there had been no perjury in his mouth.

Yahweh has been pleased to crush him with suffering.
If he offers his life in atonement,
he shall see his heirs, he shall have a long life
and through him what Yahweh wishes will be done.

His soul's anguish over
he shall see the light and be content.
By his sufferings shall my servant justify many,
taking their faults on himself.

Hence I will grant whole hordes for his tribute,
he shall divide the spoil with the mighty,
for surrendering himself to death
and letting himself be taken for a sinner,
while he was bearing the faults of many
and praying all the time for sinners.

In spite of all the energy we expend trying not to suffer, we do suffer. In spite of all the effort we make to blind ourselves to the sufferings of others, we see their pain. Not only do we observe suffering in others and personally experience it ourselves, but also we somehow receive an inner sense of goodness and growth from suffering.

No doubt, suffering is a mysterious, compelling, human reality.

The earliest, and probably the most profound, statement on human suffering in all of literature is the Song of the Suffering Servant found in the book of Isaiah. In his writing, Isaiah, one of the greatest prophets and poets of the Jewish Scriptures, brought to the Jewish people a message of their deliverance from bondage by a God of tender compassion. It is a message of hope for a displaced people who have undergone the total collapse of their nation, the loss of their religious center, and utter homelessness in a land of exile. In words that transcend his own time and nation, Isaiah attempted to lead his people to discover, within their suffering, a new meaning that would carry them into the future.

The song depicts an ideal servant of Yahweh. The role of the servant is to liberate others by willingly and consciously taking upon himself or herself their pain, sin, and suffering.

While this message of Isaiah never inspired great enthusiasm among his Jewish compatriots, it does hold for humanity the way to utilize and transform the ever-present reality of human suffering.

Jesus consistently identified with and lived out of the spirit of the suffering servant of Isaiah (Mark 8:31; Matt. 17:22–23; Luke 18:31–34).

As beloved Son of God (Isa. 42:1), Jesus provides us, the people of the Christian Scriptures, with the model for suffering and the means of true servanthood through his life, his cross, and his resurrection. He empowers us to realize our own true identity and destiny in the evolutionary process of the world toward oneness in him.

As creative agents of Christ, and actively involved in moving the world forward through suffering and hard work, we are called to three specific tasks, to three labors of love (27, pp. 82–83).

The first task is to develop ourselves, to foster self-knowledge, integration, and Christian maturity. It is to embrace in trust and surrender whatever gifts or limitations we may encounter on this journey inward.

The second task flows from and complements the first. It is to extend ourselves to others in compassion, whatever their need or pain. This extension entails the hard labor of caring for others when there is no reciprocation. It means forgiving unconditionally, that is, without retaliation. It may even involve, on occasion, deliberately allowing ourselves to encounter the evil in others and to overcome it through the power of loving. This second task is a call to decisively choose for the common good, which includes a predilection for the poor and the weak among us, those who are shunned and rejected, lost and unattractive.

This extension of self means that when we personally suffer, we remain open to the possibility that our suffering is being mysteriously used to bring healing to others. This second task of loving is, in the truest sense, a work of unification, the laying down of one's life for others (John 15:13).

The first and second tasks give rise to the third task, which is to allow oneself to be shaped by the working of the spirit within, rather than to be driven by egotistical desires or compulsive perfectionism. It is to become Christ-centered through a total surrender of our lives to God.

Teilhard de Chardin speaks of these three tasks as an interconnected dynamic process and calls them centration, decentration, and surcentration.

The tasks correspond to the threefold dynamic of the paschal mystery: the life, the death, and the resurrection of Jesus.

In the Song of the Suffering Servant we hear the spirit and prayer of Jesus as he surrenders to the love that has forever transformed the deepest yearnings of our hearts.

Such is the mystery of humankind, and it is a great one, as seen by believers in the light of Christian revelation. Through Christ and in Christ, the riddles of sorrow and death grow meaningful. Apart from his gospel, they overwhelm us. Christ has risen, destroying death by His death. He has lavished life upon us so that, as sons and daughters in the Son, we can cry out in the Spirit: Abba! (1, The Church in the Modern World, para. 22, p. 222)

Suggested Approach to Prayer: Servant of the Spirit

+ *Daily prayer pattern:* (See pages 1 and 2.)
I quiet myself and relax in the presence of God.
I declare my dependency on God.

+ *Grace:* I ask to enter deeply, fully into the Spirit of Jesus' self-emptying, surrendering love.

+ *Method:* Meditative Reading, as on page 5.
In stillness I approach the servant song of Isaiah. Slowly I read the words of Isaiah, quietly aware of the gifts that have been given to me as I prayerfully walked with Jesus through his passion.

As I make my way prayerfully through the song, verse by verse, I am receptive to the powerful images of the servant. I allow these images to take on form and shape within me.

If any image particularly resonates within me, I stay with it, drawing from it whatever consolation or insight it nurtures.

Focusing on the theme of the song, through suffering to glory, I enter into the spirit of the servant. Prayerfully, I reflect on Jesus coming into his glory.

+ *Closing:* (Review the Colloquy section on page 10.)
I speak to Christ, heart to heart, of my thanks to him and my desire to live in his Spirit.

I close by praying the prayer, Soul of Christ, page 138.

+ *Review of Prayer:* I write my own offering and commitment to Christ.

Appendix 1: Additional Prayers

Soul of Christ

Jesus, may all that is you flow into me.
May your body and blood be my food and drink.
May your passion and death be my strength and life.
Jesus, with you by my side enough has been given.
May the shelter I seek be the shadow of your cross.
Let me not run from the love which you offer,
    but hold me safe from the forces of evil.
On each of my dyings shed your light and your love.
Keep calling to me until that day comes,
    when with your saints, I may praise you forever.

(30, p. 3)

Letting Go

To a dear one about whom I have been concerned.
I behold the Christ in you.
I place you lovingly in the care of the Father.
I release you from my anxiety and concern.
I let go of my possessive hold on you.
I am willing to free you to follow the dictates
     of your indwelling Lord.
I am willing to free you to live your life
     according to your best light and understanding.
Husband, wife, child, friend—
I no longer try to force my ideas on you,
     my ways on you.
I lift my thoughts above you, above the personal level.
I see you as God sees you, a spiritual being, created
     in his image, and endowed with qualities and abilities
     that make you needed, and important—not only to me but
     to God and His larger plan.
I do not bind you, I no longer believe that you do not have
     the understanding you need in order to meet life.
I bless you.
     I have faith in you,
          I behold Jesus in you.

(Author unknown; 73, p. 100)

Prayer of Hope for the World

Lord God, we come to you in our need; create in us an awareness of the massive and seemingly irreversible proportions of the crisis we face today and a sense of urgency to activate the forces of goodness.

Where there is blatant nationalism, let there be a global, universal concern;

Where there is war and armed conflict, let there be negotiation;

Where there is stockpiling, let there be disarmament;

Where people struggle toward liberation, let there be noninterference;

Where there is consumerism, let there be a care to preserve the earth's resources;

Where there is abundance, let there be a choice for a simple lifestyle and sharing;

Where there is reliance on external activism, let there be a balance of prayerful dependence on you, O Lord;

Where there is selfish individualism, let there be an openness to community;

Where there is the sin of injustice, let there be guilt, confession, and atonement;

Where there is paralysis and numbness before the enormity of the problems, let there be confidence in our collective effort.

Lord, let us not so much be concerned to be cared for as to care, not so much to be materially secure as to know that we are loved by you. Let us not look to be served, but to place ourselves at the service of others whatever cost to self-interest, for it is in loving vulnerability that we, like Jesus, experience the fullness of what it means to be human. And it is in serving that we discover the healing springs of life that will bring about a new birth to our earth and hope to our world. Amen. (11, pp. 7–8)

Appendix 2: For Spiritual Directors

The passages and commentaries in this guide are keyed to the Spiritual Exercises of Saint Ignatius. The number in parentheses indicates the numbered paragraph or section as found in the original text of the Exercises.

For "The Principle and Foundation," see *Love* of the Take and Receive series. For Week 1, see *Forgiveness*; for Week 2, see *Birth* and the following:

Appendix 3: List of Approaches to Prayer

Index of Scriptural Passages

*Page numbers preceded by a bold F are in *Forgiveness: A Guide for Prayer*, Take and Receive series.
**Page numbers preceded by a bold L are in *Love: A Guide for Prayer*, Take and Receive series.
***Page numbers preceded by a bold B are in *Birth: A Guide for Prayer*, Take and Receive series.

Bibliography

1. Abbott, Walter M., ed. *The Documents of Vatican II.* New York: American Press, 1966.
2. Albright, W. F., and C. S. Mann. *Matthew.* Garden City, NY: Doubleday & Co., 1971.
3. Alighieri, Dante. *The Divine Comedy.* New York: Rinehart and Co., Inc., 1954.
4. Anderson, Bernard W. *Understanding the Old Testament.* Englewood Cliffs, NJ: Prentice-Hall, 1975.
5. Barclay, William. *The Gospel of John.* Vol. 2. Philadelphia: Westminster Press, 1975.
6. _____. *The Gospel of Luke.* Philadelphia: Westminster Press, 1975.
7. _____. *The Gospel of Mark.* Philadelphia: Westminster Press, 1975.
8. _____. *The Gospel of Matthew.* Vol. 1, Vol. 2. Philadelphia: Westminster Press, 1975.
9. _____. *The Letters to the Philippians, Colossians, and Thessalonians.* Philadelphia: Westminster Press, 1975.
10. Benoit, Pierre. *The Passion and Resurrection of Jesus Christ.* New York: Herder and Herder, 1969.
11. Bergan, Jacqueline, and Marie Schwan. *Peace.* Privately printed 1983; available through Center for Christian Renewal, Box 87, Crookston, MN 56716.
12. Bernstein, Leonard. *Kaddish.* Symphony No. 3. Columbia Recording.
13. Bridges, Robert, ed. *Poems of Gerard Manley Hopkins.* New York: Oxford University Press, 1948.
14. Brown, Raymond. *A Crucified Christ in Holy Week.* Collegeville, MN: The Liturgical Press, 1986.
15. _____. *The Gospel According to John XII–XXI.* Garden City, NY: Doubleday & Co., 1966.
16. _____, et al. *The Jerome Biblical Commentary.* Englewood Cliffs, NJ: Prentice-Hall, 1968.
17. Brueggemann, Walter. *The Prophetic Imagination.* Philadelphia: Fortress Press, 1978.

18. Caird, G. B. *Saint Luke.* London: Penguin Books, 1963.
19. Cowan, Marian, and John C. Futrell. *The Spiritual Exercises of St. Ignatius of Loyola: A Handbook for Directors.* New York: Le Jacq Publishing, 1982.
20. Crossman, Dominic M. "The Gospel of Jesus Christ." Stonebridge Priory, Lake Bluff, IL. Mimeographed notes. 1963.
21. de Mello, Anthony. *Sadhana, A Way to God.* Saint Louis: The Institute of Jesuit Sources, 1978.
22. _____. *Wellsprings.* Garden City, NY: Doubleday & Co., 1985.
23. Doore, Gary. "The Dynamics of Transformation," *The American Theosophist.* 74 (May 1986).
24. Eliade, Mircea. *The Sacred and the Profane.* New York: Harcourt, Brace, & World, Inc., 1957.
25. English, John. *Choosing Life.* New York: Paulist Press, 1978.
26. _____. *Spiritual Freedom.* Guelph, Ontario: Loyola House, 1974.
27. Faricy, Robert. *The Spirituality of Teilhard de Chardin.* Minneapolis: Winston Press, 1981.
28. Fenton, J.C. *Saint Matthew.* London: Penguin Books, 1963.
29. Fitzmyer, Joseph. *The Gospel According to Luke X–XXIV.* Garden City, NY: Doubleday & Co., 1985.
30. Fleming, David. *The Spiritual Exercises of St. Ignatius: A Literal Translation and a Contemporary Reading.* Saint Louis: The Institute of Jesuit Sources, 1978.
31. Fox, Matthew. *Breakthrough.* Garden City, NY: Image Books, 1977.
32. _____. *Original Blessing.* Santa Fe, NM: Bear and Co., 1983.
33. Getty, Mary Ann. *Philippians and Philemon.* Wilmington, DE: Michael Glazier, 1980.
34. Gill, Jean. *Images of My Self.* New York: Paulist Press, 1982.
35. Gibran, Kahlil. *Lazarus and His Beloved.* Greenwood, CT: New York Graphic Society, Ltd., 1973.
36. Harrington, Wilfred. *Mark.* Wilmington, DE: Michael Glazier, 1979.
37. Harriot, John. "Himself He Cannot Save." *The Way.* 10 (October 1970): 318–326.
38. John Paul II. *On the Christian Meaning of Suffering.* Washington, DC: USCC, 1984.

39. Jung, Carl G. *Aion.* Princeton, NJ: Princeton University Press, 1959.
40. _____. *Man and His Symbols.* New York: Valor Publications, 1964.
41. _____. *The Visions Seminars*, Book 1, 2. Switzerland: Spring Publications, 1976.
42. Küng, Hans. *On Being a Christian.* Garden City, NY: Doubleday & Co., 1976.
43. La Verdiere, Eugene. *Luke.* Wilmington, DE: Michael Glazier, 1980.
44. Luke, Helen M. *Woman: Earth and Spirit.* New York: Crossroads, 1985.
45. McBrien, Richard P. *Catholicism, Vol. 1, 2.* Minneapolis: Winston Press, 1980.
46. McGann, Diarmuid. *The Journeying Self.* New York: Paulist Press, 1985.
47. McKenzie, John. *Dictionary of the Bible.* Milwaukee: Bruce Publishing Co., 1965.
48. _____. *Second Isaiah.* Garden City, NY: Doubleday & Co., 1968.
49. McPalin, James. *John.* Wilmington, DE: Michael Glazier, 1979.
50. Magaña, José. *A Strategy for Liberation.* Hicksville, NY: Exposition Press, 1974.
51. Marsh, John. *St. John.* London: Penguin Books, 1968.
52. Meier, John P. *Matthew.* Wilmington, DE: Michael Glazier, 1980.
53. Moltmann, Jürgen, and Johann Metz. *Meditations on the Passion.* New York: Paulist Press, 1979.
54. National Conference of Catholic Bishops. *The Sacramentary.* New York: Catholic Books Publishing Co., 1974.
55. Neumann, Erick. *The Great Mother.* Princeton, NJ: Princeton University Press, 1963.
56. Nineham, D. E. *Mark.* Baltimore: Penguin Books, 1963.
57. Oesterreicher, John M. ed. *The Bridge.* New York: Pantheon Books, 1955.
58. O'Neill, Eugene. *Lazarus Laughed* in *The Plays of Eugene O'Neill.* New York: Random House, 1954. 273–376.
59. Paoli, Arturo. *Freedom to be Free.* Maryknoll, NY: Orbis Books, 1973.
60. Peck, M. Scott. *People of the Lie.* New York: Simon & Schuster, Inc., 1983.
61. Pennington, M. Basil. *Centering Prayer.* Garden City, NY: Image Books, 1982.

62. Perkins, Pheme. *Resurrection*. Garden City, NY: Doubleday & Co., 1984.
63. Rahner, Karl. *Foundations of Christian Faith*. New York: The Seabury Press, 1978.
64. _____. *Spiritual Exercises*. New York: Herder and Herder, 1956.
65. Rollings, Wayne G. *Jung and the Bible*. Atlanta: John Knox Press, 1983.
66. Sanford, John A. *The Kingdom Within*. New York: Paulist Press, 1970.
67. Scullion, John. *Isaiah 40–66*. Wilmington, DE: Michael Glazier, 1982.
68. Stanley, David M. *A Modern Spiritual Approach to the Spiritual Exercises*. Saint Louis: The Institute of Jesuit Sources, 1971.
69. Tannehill, Robert C. *A Mirror for Disciples: A Study of the Gospel of Mark*. Nashville: Disciples Resources, 1977.
70. Taylor, Vincent. *The Gospel According to St. Mark*. New York: St. Martin's Press, 1966.
71. Teilhard de Chardin, Pierre. *The Divine Milieu*. New York: Harper and Row, 1966.
72. Ulanov, Ann and Barry. *Primary Speech: A Psychology of Prayer*. Atlanta: John Knox Press, 1982.
73. Veltri, John. *Orientations, Vol. 1: A Collection of Helps for Prayer*. Guelph, Ontario: Loyola House, 1979.
74. _____. *Orientations, Vol. 2, Annotation 19: Tentative Edition*. Guelph, Ontario: Loyola House, 1981.
75. von Franz, Marie-Louise. *Interpretation of Fairy Tales*. Dallas: Spring Publications, 1982.
76. von le Fort, Gertrud. *The Wife of Pilate*. Milwaukee: Bruce Publishing Co., 1957.
77. Welch, John. *Spiritual Pilgrims*. New York: Paulist Press, 1982.
78. Whitmont, Edward. *Return of the Goddess*. New York: Crossroads, 1984.
79. Woodman, Marion. *Addiction to Perfection*. Toronto: Inner City Books, 1982.
80. _____. *The Pregnant Virgin*. Toronto: Inner City Books, 1985.

To Our Readers:

It would be helpful to us, as we prepare to write the subsequent volumes of this series of guides for prayer, if you would be willing to respond to the following questions, and send your response to us.

Thank You.

Jacqueline
Marie

_ _

Please check the appropriate answers and add your comments.

1. I used the guide for prayer
    _____ regularly over a period of _____ (weeks or months).
    _____ irregularly.
    Comment:

2. I found the format (i.e., cover design, paper, type, layout)
    _____ helpful to my prayer.
    _____ unhelpful to my prayer.
    Comment:

3. I found the commentaries
    _____ helpful for entering into prayer.
    _____ difficult to understand.
    Comment:

4. The commentaries that were most helpful were on pages _____
    _____

5. I (used or did not use) the approaches to prayer.
    Comment:

6. What I liked best about the guide for prayer is _____
    _____

7. The following changes or additions would make the guide for prayer more helpful: _____
    _____

_____
(Signature optional)

Mail to Center for Christian Renewal at Jesuit Retreat House, 4800 Fahrnwald Road, Oshkosh, WI 54901.